GOD
helps those
who help themselves

by
Hanna Kroeger

I dedicate this book to
the protector of America,

St. Michael,

and to his
Army of Torchbearers.
Rev. Hanna Kroeger

Copyright 1984
by
Hanna Kroeger Publications

1-800-225-8787

5th Printing 1997

Emblem on front:
Indian Wheel with the Heart of Jesus

Drawings by Vernelle Hemmat

ISBN 1-883713-11-0

TABLE OF CONTENTS

INTRODUCTION

The future belongs to those nations who are willing and capable to adopt the science of nutrition, and take full advantage of its teachings.
Dr. G. von Wendt (Sweden)

What Is Holistic Health?

Webster's Third International Dictionary defines "holistic" as "emphasizing the organic or functional relation between parts and wholes, rather than an atomistic approach." In relation to health this means recognizing that all disease processes involve the whole person. Within the physical dimension, disease in one system of the body affects the other systems. Similarly, imbalance in any one dimension of existence—physical, mental, spiritual or social—affects the other dimensions.

One reason holistic health is hard to pin down is that it represents an attitude toward health and healing, rather than specific treatments, therapies or things to do. This attitude is one which emphasizes wellness, preventive care, the responsibility of each of us for our own well-being and the need to recognize that we are not just a collection of mechanical parts but an integrated system with physical, mental, spiritual and social aspects which function in a holistic way.

What is holistic health? You hear the term a lot these days but few people seem to know what it means. As Dr. Norman Shealy, President of the American Holistic Medical Association, says, "Holistic medicine is like God. You can't quite put your finger on it . . . it's everywhere . . . and everything."

"This is Wholism: living each moment and experience to the hilt, with full mind awareness, spirit awareness; letting oneself be washed and cleansed by the pure stream of thankfulness and appreciation" (Fran Atkinson).

And Jesus said, "I make you whole" which means all facilities of all dimensions together. The physical body is dependent on your emotional faculties and your mental outlook is the watchtower.

How to Perform Your Own Miracle Healing

Health is balance of all aspects of your being—physical, mental and spiritual.

When it comes to balancing your own health, you always let someone else do it. You can manage and balance your own household, you do fine in your own business, you manage and balance your environment, you balance your checkbook, but when it comes to balancing your health, you quit. Why? Because you shy away from the work it takes to balance your body chemistry. When it comes to your own thinking and emotions you quit and go to a psychiatrist, counselor, your minister, your friends, the card reader, the palm reader, the tea leaf reader or the crystal ball gazer when you yourself could do a much better job. Of course, you need tools to do so and this book will give you the tools to help. The daring is yours, the work is yours, the determination is yours, but God is with those who help themselves and the Lord is with you.

There are seven fundamental causes of illness in the spiritual and emotional realm and seven causes in the physical realm. Usually they are not clear-cut. They are interwoven and one has to diligently undo the many knots one by one to bring back balance. Balance is the key word of nature, balance is the key word of health.

Women in Healing

As long as mankind has existed it was the woman who placed the patch of herbs on her soldier's arm. It was the woman with the basket of food and liniments who eased the sores and sufferings made by men. It was the women who entered the prisons, the schools and the hospitals, regardless of what people thought and said, to ease the pressures of manmade society for the less fortunate.

Women were always healers—naturally born healers. They hold the crying child and soothe their needs (psychiatrist). They dig out the thorn from the finger (surgeon). They ease the fever (internist). They dress the sores and bathe their beloved ones in herbs (herbalist). They dry the tears (minister).

They practice medicine without a license every day of their lives to help their fellow men, their families and their friends. This is woman's right, this is woman's concern. Who can take it away? Men have tried and failed. They will try again and again and will fail as long as you stand on your womanly right and don't go over the fence to seek the men's rights which are labeled Classical, Chemical or Mechanics.

2

CHAPTER I

Neglect
as a
Cause of Ill Health

NEGLECT

Neglect is one of the seven physical causes of ill health and we all neglect our bodies' needs. It is our fault that we do not educate ourselves about the "stuff" we are made of. Did we have our daily vitamins today? Did we do deep inhaling and exhaling? Did we sleep enough? All of these things are essential and we are the only ones to decide if we want to neglect our body and become a burden to our beloved ones or if we want to do our part to stay well. This is our choice and our choice alone.

MINERALS

Before there were vitamins, before there was food, before there was life, there were minerals. Minerals are the real stuff we are made of and they act as building stones to all cells in our bodies.

CALCIUM: Calcium is a most valuable mineral for the growing person and is of great benefit to those recovering from illnesses. The bones of the body are mainly composed of calcium and this element gives tone to the muscles while lack of it leads to decay in the bones and teeth. The human body contains more calcium than any other mineral, over 90 percent of which is deposited in bones and teeth to keep them strong and hard. The remainder is essential for healthy blood, a regular heartbeat and the health of the nervous system. Calcium deficiency is generally characterized by muscle cramps, numbness and tingling in arms and legs. Extra calcium is a highly regarded treatment for osteoporosis, arthritis and rheumatism.

Adequate calcium means:
  • Strength and energy
  • Decision making
  • Invention and good thought production

Inadequate calcium means:
  • Stuttering   • Inferiority complex
  • Stammering   • Soft bones
  • Prolapses   • Sore tissue
  • Sores

Calcium cannot be absorbed if iodine is missing.

4

ZINC: Commonly known zinc benefits often overshadow the mineral's other important duties. It is vital in the absorption and action of many vitamins. It is a component of insulin and is necessary for proper skin, nail and hair growth and appearance. Zinc is also crucial for the speedy, healthy healing of cuts and burns. Deficiency indications include:

- Stretch marks on the skin
- White spots on the fingernails
- Impaired sexual functioning
- Fatigue
- Prolonged healing of wounds

Zinc is needed in diabetes, hearing and brain functioning.

CHROMIUM: A trace mineral whose daily requirements have just recently been recognized, chromium has a crucial role to play in human health. Chromium is responsible for the metabolism of glucose into energy and can boost the effectiveness of insulin. A lack of chromium can result in fatigue, energy loss and blood sugar imbalance and the symptoms of hypoglycemia, hpyerglycemia and diabetes. Chromium is routinely deficient in modern American diets and since we absorb less as we grow older, maintaining proper levels is very difficult.

COPPER: Copper is necessary for proper iron absorption, bone growth and health and the production of RNA in the body's cells. Deficiencies are rare but a lack of copper can cause anemia and edema. On the other hand, since copper competes with zinc in the body, too much copper can precipitate a zinc deficiency.

IODINE: Iodine is required for the proper functioning of the thyroid gland. Iodine plays a major role in regulating the production of energy and stimulating the rate of metabolism. Iodine deficiencies may lead to obesity, sluggishness, slowed mental reactions and hardening of the arteries.

MAGNESIUM: Magnesium is a powerful agent in the elimination of waste matter from the system. Magnesium deficiencies are quite common with symptoms being nervousness, muscle twitches, confusion and the formation of calcium deposits. Due to its importance within the central nervous system, magnesium has a reputation as a calming, relaxing substance.

IRON: Iron carries oxygen from the lungs to all parts of the body. It gives strength to the nerves and muscles and makes the blood rich and pure. Deficiencies commonly include such symptoms as chronic fatigue, pale complexion, constipation, hair loss and anemia.

SODIUM: Sodium is a necessary constituent of the gastric juices and is found in all fluids in the body. It is valuable for general elimination of acids from the system. Sodium keeps other minerals soluble in blood and is involved in muscle expansion and contraction. Most people get too much sodium which can cause dizziness, water retention and the loss of potassium.

POTASSIUM: Potassium is required for generating the electric and magnetic forces in the body for rebuilding tissues, flesh, bones and muscles. It gives flexibility to the muscles. Potassium is necessary for normal growth, helps regulate the heartbeat and encourages the kidneys to flush out body wastes. Symptoms of deficiency include heart problems, poor reflexes, edema, dry skin and poor muscle tone. Supplemental potassium can balance out excess salt, lower high blood pressure, reduce blood sugar levels and relieve water retention.

MANGANESE: As an enzyme activator and catalyst, manganese provides nourishment to the nerves and brain. A deficiency can prevent excess sugar from being removed from the blood, impair muscle coordination and cause fatigue and female disorders.

PHOSPHORUS: Phosphorus is a stimulant to the nerves and brain. Without this element the bones deteriorate and lung tissues become prey to infections which, under healthy conditions, are destroyed by phosphoric acid.

SILICON: Silicon absorbs gases in the body, especially in the bowels, and is a substance in the cells of connective tissues. Silicon is needed for vitamin B assimilation.

SELENIUM: Selenium has been the subject of much recent interest and favorable publicity. It is highly valued for its natural antioxidant powers and is known to retard aging and help preserve tissue elasticity by neutralizing harmful oxidative reactions in the cells. Research into selenium's benefits indicates that it can be helpful in inhibiting tumor formation and heart disease. The main deficiency symptom is premature aging but deficiencies have also been linked to infertility and lowered intelligence. In spite of its importance to health, many Americans are selenium deficient.

Two Kinds of Minerals: Organic and Inorganic

The body is composed of both organic and inorganic elements and the organic predominates. The organic cannot perform its proper functioning without the inorganic. Dr. William A. Albrecht, Professor Emeritus of Soils, College of Agriculture, University of Missouri, the dean of a lifetime of research on trace minerals in soil and their effects on plants, animals and people, states that although some minerals are insoluble (inorganic), they become soluble upon coming in contact with the mucous membranes of the body.

Thus, Dr. Albrecht says, the insoluble can become available through the exchange transformation to water and, hence, can become available as nourishment. He adds that natural plant growth emphasizes the fact that the inorganic (insoluble), as well as the highly organic (soluble), are both biochemically active. Dr. Albrecht adds that chelation may explain why nature can transform an insoluble element into a biochemically active one.

Any biochemistry textbook will tell you that both organic and inorganic elements occur in the body and both are needed to rebuild the constant wear and tear and degeneration of the body. Phosphorus, for instance, is not only present in inorganic combinations (such as bones, teeth, blood, etc.) but in many organic combinations. Inorganic and organic elements are in equilibrium with each other and come from the food we eat and the beverages we drink. In addition, many enzymes require small quantities of inorganic elements for their activity.

Inorganic minerals are needed for your electromagnetic body as well as building and rebuilding bones, tissues and the entire you.

Today only 4 or 5 percent of our bodies are composed of minerals (the rest is mostly water) but this small percentage is really the stuff of which we are made. Minerals make our teeth and bones hard and give shape and function to our bodies' cells. Minerals also act as catalysts for biological functioning, digestion, muscle response and hormone production.

One of the best examples of the effect of minerals on health is that of the Hunzas. Their water is so full of minerals, largely inorganic, that it is not only murky but the sediment settles at the bottom of the glass when it is allowed to stand. Yet these people have been known to have the best health of any people in the world.

Foods are often grown on exhausted, mineral deficient soil and are then subjected to further depletion by refining and cooking. Moreover, as we grow older, the body's ability to absorb minerals decreases. Medications, illnesses and poor eating habits further hamper proper absorption of minerals so that most of us suffer from at least some mineral deficiencies.

ENZYMES

Enzymes are found in all living cells, including raw foods or those that are cooked at a temperature lower than 118 degrees Fahrenheit. Enzymes begin to perish when the temperature increases beyond this. The degree of enzyme destruction is a function of time and temperature.

Enzymes are needed to help control all mental and physical functions. Enzymes work with other substances such as minerals, vitamins and proteins. Enzymes help extract the minerals from food. Enzymes work with vitamins in every chemical reaction inside and outside the cells. Enzymes aid in transforming proteins into amino acids. (Protein does not perform its function unless broken down into amino acids.) Enzymes rule over all other nutrients. Enzymes are responsible for nearly every facet of life and health and far outweigh the importance of every other nutrient.

Many experts believe that enzyme deficiency is a forerunner to disease and that nearly all people, because of improper diet over the years, need to replenish their enzyme supply. Enzymes are, therefore, justified as a supplemental dietary substance just as we add vitamins and minerals to our diet.

VITAMINS

Vitamins are most fascinating. They can give strength and, when properly directed, can heal the oddest conditions the body can display.

That we don't know enough is our very own neglect and our very own problem. Don't blame anyone else. You are in your body, you know and feel where it is weak or aching, so do something about it.

Vitamins are not drugs! With enough minerals and a proper working digestive tract the human body is able to manufacture vitamins all by itself. A properly functioning digestive tract makes all of the B vitamins we need.

The body can manufacture vitamins but not minerals.

- The right collarbone manufactures vitamin A.
- The left collarbone manufactures vitamin B$_{12}$.
- The floating rib manufactures vitamin E.
- The healthy digestive system manufactures all of the B vitamins.
- The tailbone manufactures vitamin C.
- The red bone marrow manufactures vitamin K.
- The left leg manufactures linoleic acid.
- The small intestine manufactures interferon.
- The tip of the sternum is concerned with the right kind of vitamin D.

However, in this day and age when stress problems are prevalent, the miracle manufacturing plant in our body cannot function properly without outside help.

We do not need as many calories as our hard working ancestors needed. And besides, their food was mostly homegrown. No additives or preservatives were in the food. Food also stays preserved in our guts. In the past, food did not undergo freezing processes (which takes vitamin E out).

There were no fluorescent lights, which rob vitamin A, and no pollution, which is known to rob vitamin C. Therefore, we need vitamins and *I mean every one of us.*

A (CAROTENE): Eyes, teeth, bones, skin, soft tissues, dry skin, nose, throat, mouth, digestive tract, male and female genital organs, pimples, colds, sinuses, tonsils, bronchial tubes, allergies, growth, hair, heartburn, kidney stones, gallstones. 1 mg per 50 pounds of body weight. (This seems unrealistically low.)

C (ASCORBIC ACID): Body cells, ligaments, arteries, veins, tissues, bones, pyorrhea, bad teeth, allergies, diphtheria, influenza, dysentery, measles, mumps, shingles, fever blisters, chicken pox, polio, bruises, eyes, restlessness, irritability, healing, complexion, nails, blood, resistance to shock, fights infection. 500 mg daily.

D: All glands, reproduction, distributes calcium and phosphorus, makes skin breathe, activated by sunshine and energy. Lack of D causes rickets (soft bone disease), acne, arthritis, nearsightedness. 500 IU daily.

E: Muscle tissue, reproductive glands, sterility, miscarriages, testicular degeneration, liver, cerebral palsy, epilepsy, nerves, mental disorders, heart, fertility, life span, pituitary glands, hormone production, adrenal and sex glands, bursitis, rheumatism, varicose veins, circulation, softens scar tissue, ulcers, wounds, burns. 400 IU daily.

K: Blood clotting. 100 mg daily.

B_1 (THIAMINE CHLORIDE): Nerves, oversensitivity, memory, morale, digestion, constipation, nausea, appetite, heart, irritability, thyroid gland, tiredness, stress, metabolism of fats and carbohydrates. 25 mg daily.

B_2 (RIBOFLAVIN): Metabolism of starches and sugar, skin, vision, reproduction, longevity, lactation, digestion, athlete's foot, allergies. 25 mg daily.

NIACIN: Liver, nerves, soft tissues, skin, burning of starches and sugars, gums, circulation, digestion, dual personality, cowardliness. Niacinamide is another name for niacin. 100 mg daily.

B_6 (PYRIDOXINE): Paralysis, muscle tone, nerves, acne, conserves protein, intolerance to sunshine, dizziness, insomnia, fatigue, palsy, joint stiffness. 25 mg daily.

FOLATE/FOLIC ACID: Red blood cells, anemia, poor appetite. 10 mg daily.

B_{12} (COBALAMIN): Pernicious anemia, nerve degeneration, growth, asthma, skin disorders, blood, fatigue, listlessness, paleness, unclear thinking. 500 mcg daily.

BIOTIN: Mental health, dry skin, poor appetite, muscles, nausea, mental depression. 3 mg daily.

PANTOTHENIC ACID: Growth, hair, wrinkles, stress, nerves, digestion, anemia, arthritis, constipation, stomach ulcers, adrenal glands, water retention, edema. 100 mg daily.

CHOLINE: Metabolism of fats, liver, kidneys, spleen, nerves, muscles, diabetes, gallbladder, arteriosclerosis (hardening of arteries), cancer, fatigue, skin, anti-grey hair. Is valuable in all cases of dyspepsia and disorders of the stomach. 250 mg daily.

INOSITOL: Growth, anti-grey hair, hair loss, liver, intestines, muscles, utilization of vitamins V and E, brain functioning, heart and nerve muscle function. 250 mg daily.

RUTIN (BIOFLAVONOIDS): Small blood vessels, high blood pressure, strokes, ankle swelling, allergies. 50 mg daily.

PARA-AMINOBENZOIC ACID (PABA): Anti-grey hair, sterility, thyroid gland, all other glands, arthritis, hormone activation. 100 mg daily.

F: Unsaturated fatty acids, lubricates all cells, skin, nails, hair. Lack of F causes bronchial asthma, hay fever, baldness, acne. 100 mg daily.

CELL SALTS (TISSUE SALTS)

In our search for truth we have to consider one branch of food additives—the cell salt—found, invented and documented by Dr. Schuessler 100 years ago. This genius found that by supplying the minimum dosage of twelve important minerals, the body responds extremely favorable.

Schuessler's tissue salts have a specific place in supplying the body and its cells with the needed building materials.

Tissue salts, also called cell salts, are only vibrations of twelve fundamental minerals. But, being of vibrations *alone*, they nourish the finer body and rebuild the aura. They also stimulate and spark into action already present minerals. Cell salts spark the entire metabolism by bringing together and catalyzing organic and inorganic mineral supplies.

11

Twelve Tissue Salts:

1) *CALCIUM FLUORIDE:* Calcium fluoride deals with the treatment of ailments connected with bones, decaying teeth, blood and relaxed conditions of muscle fibers such as falling womb, abortion, corpulence and enlarged heart muscles.

2) *CALCIUM PHOSPHATE:* Calcium phosphate is noted for its effect on the skeletal frame of the body—delayed dentition, decaying teeth, bone deformities and other skeletal affections. It is a valuable remedy for expectant mothers, especially for women who are incapable of carrying to full term. It has a sedative effect on the body, just like that of lime on the soil. It forms part of the blood corpuscles and gastric acid and is, therefore, effective in the treatment of anemia and gastritis.

3) *CALCIUM SULFATE:* Calcium sulfate is known as a blood purifier and healer, causing the discharge of decaying, organic matter. It is indicated in boils, ulcers, abscesses and skin affections. It is normally used in conjunction with *Silica.*

4) *FERRIC PHOSPHATE (IRON):* Ferric phosphate is known as the oxygen carrier and could, therefore, be helpful in many illnesses. It is indicated in all inflammatory conditions and all cases characterized by a rise in temperature, such as fevers, colds, coughs, croup, bronchitis, pleurisy, measles, chicken pox and pneumonia. It is also applicable in all anemic cases, iron being a constituent of the hemoglobin part of the red blood corpuscles.

5) *KALIUM MURIATE (POTASSIUM CHLORIDE):* Kalium muriate is indicated in cases of long-standing, sluggish conditions. Its symptoms are characterized by a white coating of the tongue, such as in diphtheria, croup, pneumonia, etc., and by thick white discharges affecting the skin and mucous membranes. It is useful when the blood tends to thicken and form clots.

6) *KALIUM PHOSPHATE (POTASSIUM PHOSPHATE):* Kalium phosphate is associated with all nervous affections such as nervous headaches and irritability, in fact, all ailments originating from nervous tension, such as fretfulness, hysteria, neuralgia, etc. Children's tantrums can be an indication of a deficiency of this cell salt.

7) *KALIUM SULFATE (POTASSIUM SULFATE):* Kalium sulfate is also an oxygen carrier and is indicated when there is a feeling of stuffiness or a need for fresh air. It is noted for skin affections characterized by a yellow discharge and has been found helpful in maintaining a healthy scalp and hair.

8) *MAGNESIUM PHOSPHATE:* Cases where this salt is indicated are characterized by spasmodic pains of the teeth, head, stomach and abdomen. It is helpful to relieve muscular twitching and is noted for relieving nervous affections producing convulsions, cramps, menstrual pains and any other sharp twinges of pain. Flatulence can be relieved by this cell salt, making it a useful remedy for colic.

9) *NATRIUM MURIATE (SODIUM CHLORIDE):* Although this is, in fact, common salt, it is capable of correcting cases resulting from excessive use of common salt. Its indication is associated with body fluids and malnutrition, such as coryza, and it is known as the water distributing tissue salt. A natrium muriate deficiency must be considered when there is excessive dryness or moisture in any part of the body or when there is an indication of an imbalance of the water system, such as eyes tearing, abnormal salivation, constipation, etc.

10) *NATRIUM PHOSPHATE (SODIUM PHOSPHATE):* Natrium phosphate is known as the acid neutralizer. It is useful in cases of worms, acidity, heartburn and regurgitation, in fact, all gastric derangements. It has also been found helpful in cases of stiffness and swelling of joints.

11) *NATRIUM SULFATE (SODIUM SULFATE):* This salt is indicated in all cases of biliousness, gallstones, nausea and vomiting. It is known to eliminate excess water in the system which may contain toxic matter. It is essential to a healthy liver.

12) *SILICA (SILICIS OXIDE):* Silica is a cleanser and eliminator. It is noted for the relief of boils, ulcers, abscesses and glandular swellings, in fact, it promotes suppuration in all cases of tumors. Its action is rather sturdy but deep-seated. It could effectively be used in alternation with calcium sulfate.

THE IMPORTANCE OF
EXERCISE, WATER AND SUNSHINE

Exercise

Our body needs exercise. The lymphatic system does not work without sufficient exercise. Protein assimilation depends on a properly working lymphatic system. So protein assimilation depends on exercise. Did you walk today? Climb your stairway—do it an extra time tonight just for exercise—or use your trampoline a few minutes at a time. Go out into the sunshine and bring the sun back into your house with a smile on your face.

Water

Water is an important component of the cells and tissues. It keeps tissues soft and pliable and acts as a solvent of gases, foods, etc., permitting diffusion of these substances in the body. It is the medium of transport for food absorbed from the alimentary canal. Absorbed food is carried from the alimentary canal in the watery blood plasma to all parts of the body. Water enables glands to manufacture their particular secretions and assists in regulating body temperature. Harmful waste is carried in solution to excretory organs.

Your body consists of 90 percent water. Water is the most important "food" intake. Too little attention is placed on this fact. Fluid is needed for assimilation and transmutation of minerals and vitamins. Foods and oxygen cannot be used without fluids. Therefore, I urge you to drink healthful fluids, such as fresh juices, good water, herbal teas and buttermilk, instead of liquor, alcohol, soda pop and junk drinks.

To make positive vion rich water (vions are ions of the water), take two horseshoe magnets and place them around a jar of water so they repel each other. Have the positive to negative poles with the glass jar in the middle.

Sunshine, Negative Ions and Full Spectrum Lighting

For the past 50 years, our society has lived and worked more and more inside. No one has ever calculated the side effects of this behavior as a whole. All of us are lacking sunshine and negative ions which nature provides so freely.

What about bringing these into our homes? We know about the healthful effects of negative ions. You sleep deeper and are more rested. You are more alert at your work. You live a happier life. Airborne allergies vanish. Asthma is lessened. Behavior troubled children are calmed down and sleep a restful night.

The trouble with us is that we hear of negative ions and we think that more is better. Realize that, if you can read comfortably with a reading lamp with 75 watts, you cannot read when you put 10,000 watts into your lamp.

So it is with negative ions. If you overcharge your room, your body cannot absorb or utilize the unnatural balance of negative ions. Ask the author for more information.

We all agree that we do not have enough sunlight in our homes. Full spectrum lighting fixtures (a combination of black light with chroma light) truly are remarkable. It is sunshine in your house. Combine full spectrum lighting with negative ions and you've brought the outdoors inside. The following results of concrete studies give reasons for changing to a full spectrum lighting system.

Hyperactivity was greatly lessened in schoolchildren under these lights, eyestrain was eliminated and substantially fewer cavities were noted, as well as fewer colds, greater muscle strength, reduction of airborne bacteria and greater visual acuity with less illumination. This type of light cures certain types of depression, combats fatigue, increases work capacity, reduces high blood pressure, reduces the amount of insulin needed by diabetics, tends to restore hormonal balance, strengthens the body's immune system, quickens the healing process, especially of bones, and the list goes on.

Man has the power to know right, to choose between good and evil and to know that his choice has made a difference. Without the light of the sun with its varied wavelengths (x-ray, ultraviolet, infrared, visible, radio, etc.), life as we know it could not exist. Light is and was that which forms the blueprint for the evolving forms of life on this planet. As our earth's atmosphere filters the sun's rays, she provides only a specific aggregate of light wavelengths to reach her surface.

As life evolved on this sphere, it did so under a very specific combination of wavelengths, the quality of which had the effect of enhancing or inhibiting the evolution of specific life forms. What we see today around us that we term life is the direct effect of sunlight over eons of time playing upon the environment of our planet.

The need for sunlight is much the same as our need for food and, just as through one's dietary intake of food one either nourishes or starves the body, so it is with light. Man is attuned both physiologically and psychologically to the subtle energies of light. Since the beginning of time, light has tuned the strings of our bodies to play a multitude of symphonies which we term life processes.

We need only to look to the agricultural industry to see the effect of what a change in the natural environment can do to the life processes of living things. It has been cost effective and more efficient to raise animals in a closed environment but, in doing so, man has incurred a multitude of challenges. Feeds must be fortified immensely to assure that some of the nutrients (and hopefully enough) reach the vital areas of the body to maintain an adequate health, yet disease flourishes. Multiple vaccinations against diseases that are unheard of in a natural environment have become a must. In all, performance of animals has been drastically reduced by keeping them in a closed environment.

Full spectrum lighting is an artificial lighting "system" that recreates a natural outdoor light environment at an intensity level which is safe. "System" is the word emphasized here because there are lights on the market today which claim to be "full spectrum" but which, in the true definition of the concept, are not. These other lights either do not provide a full spectrum for the length of the life of the bulb or produce more than a full spectrum of light such as the production of x-rays or radiation in the form of radio frequencies which have been shown to cause, among other things, a gross loss of muscle strength.

Unlike the animals that have been forced into living in closed environments to suit man's purpose, man himself has chosen long ago to live that way. Yet man, like his younger brothers the animals, is heir to the difficulties that arise from separating himself from the natural light environment under which he evolved.

Even the glass used to allow visible light to brighten enclosed space blocks out part of the natural spectrum of sunlight.

Dr. Richard Wurtman, the world renowned neuroendocrinologist, has pioneered contemporary research on the effects of light on living things and has traced visual pathways in humans, which are independent of the optic tract. These lead to brain centers that control, among other things, endocrine function and, hence, metabolic activity. These photoreceptors (or light sensitive receptors) in the eye respond to specific wavelengths of light found in natural sunlight and serve to regulate and reinforce normal functioning of bodily processes. In other words, the composite spectrum of normal sunlight acts like a computer card to the brain via the photoreceptors in the eyes, therefore reinforcing and stabilizing the harmony in bodily processes which have evolved over countless ages under the full spectrum influence of the sun. Many natural wavelengths of radiant energy found in sunlight that reach the surface of our planet are not even present in artificial light sources. It may be said that all artificial light sources emit a distorted sun spectrum or emit additional frequencies not found in sunlight.

This, then, results in either an overstimulation, understimulation or no stimulation at all to the photoreceptors in the eyes. Also, for those who must wear corrective eye lenses, there is available a special plastic lens which allows the full spectrum of the sun to penetrate the eye.

Most assuredly, our bodies are miraculous in their ability to adapt and recuperate under unfavorable circumstances. Yet, such is the steady pressure of this seemingly subtle influence of light that, after repeated and prolonged exposure to artificial lighting, our brain centers succumb to these distorted signals and things begin to go awry.

Full spectrum lighting, which grounds radio frequencies emitted by fluorescent lights and shields cathodes, has never shown any type of harmful effect on any living thing that evolved under the spectrum of sunlight.

This is definitely not the case with conventional fluorescent tubes, high intensity discharge lamps or metal halide lamps.

KINESIOLOGY

We are affected by everything in the environment in which we live, either positively or negatively. One of the ways that we can determine which things affect us positively or negatively is through muscle testing.

Muscle Testing

1) Have the subject stand erect, left arm relaxed at the side, right arm held out parallel to the floor with elbow straight.

2) Face the subject and place your left hand on the subject's extended right arm just above the wrist.

3) Tell the subject you are going to try to push his arm down as he resists with all his strength.

4) Now push down on his arm quickly and firmly. The idea is to push just hard enough to test the spring and bounce in the arm but not so hard that the muscle becomes fatigued. It is not a question of who is stronger but of whether the muscle can lock the shoulder joint against the push.

5) Now put the item to be tested in your patron's left hand and check again.

- If the food or item is good, the arm will lock in place and stay strong.
- If the item is not good, you will be able to push the arm down. Any food or item that muscle tests weak is not good for him. You could say that it weakens or that the subject is allergic to it.

Test all of the foods you eat. This technique is also good for vitamin and herb testing. Remember, one vitamin may test positive but, when you take a bunch of different vitamins at the same time, they may weaken you. Put all the vitamins in your left hand and test if they can be taken together.

If we don't do something about our eating habits, we'll all be sick by 1997. This is the dramatic warning given by Dr. Emanuel Cheraskin of the University of Alabama Dental School, who has authored 13

18

books on the relationship between diet and disease, which included studying what we eat and how it affects us.

Not only will the man in the street get sick but his doctor will as well. The medical profession eats the same amount of rubbish we do.

"Americans have the worst diet in the world," said Cheraskin. "And even doctors, who should know better, are not eating enough of the right foods to keep them healthy."

But the worst offenders are teen-age girls. "Teen-age boys eat a little better and get more nutrition, simply because they eat more than girls do," he explained. "People in their 30's and 40's also are busy building physical deficiencies which are bound to result in serious illness later.

"If we keep on with these eating habits, by 1997 everyone will be ill."

"There is evidence now to indicate that poor eating habits might be responsible for many more types of illnesses than science ever imagined," claimed Cheraskin.

"Even infertility, mental retardation, heart disease and cancer may be directly related to poor nutrition."

It looks like we are what we eat after all. And what we eat is usually a lot of garbage. So, if we don't do something about our diet soon, we may all wind up in the trash bin.

But there is hope. Already some of the people taking part in Cheraskin's experiments, who had damaged their health by poor eating habits, have turned their health around by a proper diet.

MENTAL AND SPIRITUAL
NEGLECT CAN CAUSE ILLNESS

Mental Attitude Is Your Responsibility

Neglect in the mental realm can cause trouble in the physical body. Inform yourself by reading or listening to ideas and alternatives, particularly because of the specializations we endure in our society nowadays.

Read a little bit every day and, in case you do not have time, listen to worthwhile tapes while you drive or do your dishes. It is said that we use only 10 percent of our brain capacities. If we do not exercise the brain, soon its potential will drop and drop and drop.

Your Spiritual Responsibility:
Do Not Neglect to Pray, to Meditate, to Contemplate!

Neglect in Spiritual Ways—Have you done your morning prayers? Did you protect your aura? Every culture and every civilization has had or has a method of protecting the human aura from foreign, undesirable influences.

The American Indians raised their arms and asked their spirits for protection not only for themselves but also for the animal kingdom and plant kingdom.

The Japanese use candles and perform candle ceremonies.

The Christians hold the cross or hold the Bible and ask for the light and its protection from Master Jesus.

All cultures realize that a neglect in protection of the spiritual body could become a vital mistake in the course of the day. In any case, I recommend strongly that you not neglect your spiritual body. By doing it only once a week on Sunday morning in church is not enough.

It is true that honest prayer makes a blue light. A blue light is a power, an energy which is of creative nature.

Bless your food and the blue light of your blessing will make your food a healing food. Bless your water and it will become a healing water. Bless your child and pray over your beloved ones and the blue light will heal the fluid which will reach the very cell and the cell will obey the light.

CAUSE AND EFFECT

Cause is in subconsciousness—the unseen.

Effect is in circumstances—the seen.

When the effect is in circumstances involving health, you can be sure that your consciousness is causing this. But how?

The key is in negativity.

What follows are ten major areas where negativity may enter consciousness. Convert this negativity to positivity and you create a consciousness of continued good health.

20

TEN COMMANDMENTS FOR
MAINTAINING PERFECT HEALTH

1) Accept criticism as the other person's problem, not yours.

2) Appreciate yourself and reaffirm your self-worth whenever necessary.

3) See the good points in circumstances. See even problems as happening for the best.

4) Rather than looking backward with sorrow, look forward with joyous expectation.

5) Rather than fretting about what you do not have, appreciate what you have.

6) Learn from mistakes so that you can convert them into triumphs.

7) Insulate yourself from distasteful surroundings through wholesome detachment.

8) Let go readily of what you no longer need and make the most of what you now attract.

9) Grow in courage and self-mastery from every circumstance.

10) Be aware of the larger consciousness of which you are a part.

These might be called the ten commandments to good health. They are beyond the physical—in the unseen world of consciousness. Observe them and enjoy perfect health. Positively.

CHAPTER II

Trauma
as a
Cause of Ill Health

SELF-CARE

This is what the self-care movement is all about. Seven hundred courses of self-help are being given in at least 40 states patterned after how to help yourself. The self-care movement has grown in a period when all authorities, including physicians, are being challenged by a skeptic public. The self-care movement suggests that we learn the risks of our particular ways of living so we can make sensible changes.

The question comes to our mind, "Does self-help work?" Yes it does. A tooth is extracted, then starts to bleed. A trip to the emergency room costs $75. A Lipton tea bag costs only two cents. Most busy physicians encourage us to practice self-care. In order for a body to be healthy we have to take care of it daily.

Since you usually act as your own doctor anyway, why not learn how to do a good job of it? We all understand that there are situations in which you need surgical and medical help. But take responsibility for your "wellness" (not sickness) by learning all you can about your body and its care.

TRAUMA

Injuries are not only accidents, injuries are also operations. An injury rocks the aura, an operation cuts the aura. An injury offsets the aura, an operation makes holes in the aura. Therefore, an aura has to be mended after it is hurt.

Shock will injure the aura. In all cases of injuries there are two things to be done: 1) heal the injured part; 2) heal the aura. In my opinion, healing the aura is almost more important and here I will tell you a most unusual story.

Mrs. Worthington was a good customer in my little store. We talked about many spiritual things. When she entered my establishment I pushed all work aside just to chat with her. She used to study with the Kahunas and the masters of Easter Island and nourished my curious mind.

One day we heard a terrible scream outside. We both rushed to see what it was. There lay a woman on the sidewalk. Obviously she had slipped. The bone of her right leg was sticking out of the skin, broken, blood oozing. We helped her into a more comfortable position.

Then I ran to call the ambulance. Looking back, I saw Mrs. Worthington kneel in front of the leg. Her big, massive body shielded the spectators from what she was doing. She swished her hands over the leg back and forth and murmured some kind of secret formula. I was so slow in finding the number of the ambulance. I could not get the answer quickly enough, it took much longer than usual. Coming out, my friend was still bent over the leg murmuring but there was no skin broken and no bone sticking out. A peaceful look on the face of the injured woman showed that there was no pain any longer.

I still thank God that the ambulance took so long and I could see the miracle happening before my eyes. The bone looked straight now, no swelling. The wound was closed and Mrs. Worthington urged the patient to move her feet. When the ambulance finally arrived we helped the woman to her feet and here she stood on both feet saying thank you to us. Later on I heard that she went home the next day because there was no more trouble.

I pulled Mrs. Worthington into the shop. "Please tell me what you did, tell me how you did it." "Oh not much," this humble woman said. "I just mended the aura of the bone and there was time enough for the bone to heal itself." "Where did you learn this?" I questioned her. "It is the teaching of the sages on Easter Island that I applied here. I really don't know much. I just learned to heal bones, that's all" she said.

This experience gave me an insight in healing, *a lesson I never will forget.*

OSTEOPATHIC MEDICINE

In a small town in Kansas a century ago, a country physician announced that he had abandoned orthodox medicine to found his own healing system. He persisted in this course despite fierce opposition from the medical profession, gained a devoted following and, thus, launched osteopathy. Founder, Dr. Andrew Taylor Still, was a colorful physician who grew up in the traditions of frontier medicine. His father, Dr. Abram Still, was a Methodist medical missionary serving Indian tribes.

Dr. Andrew Still was born on August 6, 1828, in Jonesboro, Virginia. He learned medicine from his father and later attended courses at the Kansas City College of Physicians and Surgeons. As a young man, it has been said that he roamed the prairies digging up Indian graves so that he could learn anatomy by dissecting corpses.

He served as a militia officer and hospital steward in the Civil War, then settled in Baldwin, Kansas. When three of his children died of spinal meningitis, he turned against the medical practices of the day, especially the use of massive medications, and began to devise his own system. He became convinced that spinal dislocation was a root cause of illness, creating pressures on nerves and blood vessels that either led to a direct breakdown or else so weakened the body that it lost its natural resistance to disease.

HERBS AND TRAUMA

There are some dependable herbs for trauma conditions. *Arnica Montana* has many names, such as Mountain daisy, Leopard's bane and Mountain tobacco. Arnica has bright chrome yellow flowers. The plant can reach a height of nearly two feet. Arnica is used topically (from outside). Make a strong tea and take a soft towel. Soak the towel in warm tea and apply over bruises, dislocations, corns, bunions, carbuncles, boils and insect bites. Arnica is beneficial in all injuries when it is *not an open sore or broken skin.*

For inner bruises, take arnica as a tincture or in homeopathic form (6x to 30x does a good job). When a person has had prenatal injuries, here is a surprise—an arm too short or fingers undeveloped— try arnica in high dosage IM and see miracles happen.

Another flower that acts with promptitude is the *common daisy.* When you perform unaccustomed work, such as lawn mowing or gardening, mountain climbing or too much roller skating and muscles become stiff, there is our lovely daisy. Make a brew of daisies and again take a soft towel and apply it to your sore muscles. Also, several spoonfuls of daisy tea taken by mouth is very, very helpful in stiff and sore muscles. You may have daisy tincture in your cupboard just to have it ready.

The Biblical herb *rue is* a very special one. In painfully twisted wrists, overworked tendons or painfully twisted elbows, make a concoction with rue and apply it to the painful arm. In only a few days the wrist will be normal again. Rue works on the upper part of the body.

It is the most incredible herb as an eyesight restorer. It gives the "Ray of Light" back to the aging eye. Make rue tea using 1 tsp. rue to 1 cup of water and steep 5 minutes. Drink 1 cup 2 times daily.

St. John's wort *(Hypericum perforatum)* also belongs in the "trauma medicine chest."

- It closes the lips of the wound.
- It relieves pain, particularly toothaches.
- It dissolves swelling.
- It opens obstructions.
- It repairs nerve damage.

ACUPRESSURE AND CONTACT HEALING

One of the most outstanding inventors on this earth today is Rev. Dr. Fred Houston. He is the man who found an acupressure method that works for us Westerners. His tremendous book on contact healing should be in every house. It is called *The Healing Benefits of Acupressure*. *See* Ch. VIII (Collection of Knowledge: Recommended Readings).

He gave me permission to demonstrate to you how to get rid of old traumatic conditions. Stand in front of the friend who has asked for your help. Slide your hands over his shoulder and hold the notch where the scapula attaches to the arm joint. Feel a little around and if it is sore, hold it. Let your friend close his eyes and let him experience what happens. Sometimes an old operation site starts burning or getting warm or a bone starts hurting or gets warm. Hold until all sensations are gone (between 5 and 10 minutes). That is enough for one day. If needed, repeat the next day until no more pain or warm areas are evident.

This is a terrific method to get rid of old injuries.

FOOT REFLEX MASSAGE

Foot reflex massage is a very scientific massage of the feet without using any mechanical devices. Only the hands of the therapist do the work and the healing forces can work directly. But this massage does not serve only the feet and the legs. It treats the whole human being. There are exactly localized reflex zones to all parts of the body. The treatment of these reflexes often works so well that it is without any doubt superior to any other kind of treatment. Thousands of years ago people of high culture knew about this treatment.

Every human being has reflexes in the feet but they are only painful if the related organ is either overstrained, weakened, affected or really sick. This way the therapist gets a pretty good picture of what should be treated.

Foot reflexology can prevent long suffering. It is very important to know about the reactions. They are desirable and they are a sign that a person still has enough strength to heal himself and get rid of the toxins. The reactions are individually very different. Some are disagreeable but they do not last too long and do help in re-establishing health.

The most common reactions are as follows:

- Relaxation and deeper sleep.
- Secreting more urine (cleaning blood and kidneys).
- Changes in the urine causing it to be turbid and darker.
- More bowel movements.
- Secretions from nose and throat.

Foot reflexology plays an important part in traumatic and congestive disorders.

SIMPLE TECHNIQUE FOR HICCUPS

Dr. Joseph Stapczynski, an emergency medicine specialist, advised: Take an ear swab and gently massage the back area of the roof of your mouth where it is soft and fleshy for approximately 1 minute. "If you are unsure of where this fleshy roof area begins, you can gently run your finger back along the roof of your mouth until you feel where the hard area ends and the soft area begins."

This remarkably effective technique works by actually interrupting the hiccup reflex, doctors believe. It has worked in 100 percent of patients.

CIRCULATION

First, hold in front of ears, both sides, for about 1 minute. Then, using the right hand an inch or so away from the body, make 10 clockwise circles over the heart. Then, do the same thing over the thymus, 10 times clockwise.

BONES

Our bones are very sensitive to street drugs. Years after someone has had LSD and other no-no items, the bones are, and stay, weakened. A small fall or a wrong step and a bone is broken. When I find someone with weak bones and he/she is not a senior citizen, I know that the body was abused with drugs.

To know if your bones are broken or weak, touch the 7th vertebra. If it is sore, your bones cry out for help. (Dr. Fred Houston's method.)

Bone meal, calcium orotate, vitamin C, comfrey root, oat straw tea and an oat straw mattress are all bone strengthening.

CHAPTER III

Congestion
as a
Cause of Ill Health

The Third Contributing Factor to Ill Health Is Congestion.

CONGESTION

Congestion needs short fasts and herbs. A surgeon and physician use different instruments for different procedures. We women use different fasts and different herbal teas to accomplish the cleaning out.

Have you ever been in debt? If so, you know how difficult it is to pay debts off. You have to work three times as hard, first to make a living now, second to pay back the debts and third to pay back the interest. It is the same with your body. Debts of your negligence pertaining to your body cannot be repaid with one injection or by skipping alcohol for a day or two.

To be free from pain through an injection or a pill has nothing to do with healing your body. Whoever lives against the laws of nature is losing valuable and happy years. Whoever lives with the laws of nature is on the winning side, gaining happy, healthy years in which you can help yourself and others.

DECONGEST YOUR ARTERIES

Over a quarter million aortocoronary bypass surgeries are performed in the United States every year. It is the most frequently performed major surgery in this country. Between 2 and 5 percent of aortocoronary bypass patients have complications from surgeries, including death. Many people who undergo this surgery never fully recover and are unable to return to work. This type of operation relieves the symptoms of heart disease but does not affect the causes.

"It is a sad fact that a surgical intervention constitutes an admission of failure of medical treatment. The surge of aortocoronary bypass operations gives testimony to the absence of effective medical treatment directed to alleviate or eliminate the cause underlying the disease process." Nutrition News, December 1982.

ARTERIOSCLEROSIS AND ATHEROSCLEROSIS

"My people are dying from lack of knowledge." These words from the Bible come to me as I write about how arteriosclerosis can be healed.

Arteriosclerosis is a term applied to a pathological condition in which there is thickening, hardening and loss of elasticity of the walls of blood vessels, especially the arteries; in short, it is hardening of the arteries.

Atherosclerosis takes place when arteries are blocked and the blood cannot pass through freely.

Long before it comes to a stroke and/or heart attack, the buildup in the arteries is there. It builds up over the years and arteriosclerosis is no longer a disease specific to senior citizens. Young men in their 30's or even younger show signs of trouble. Recently, researchers found arterial changes in infants. Even women, who were thought to have immunity to arterio-sclerosis, suffer more and more from this disease.

When physicians speak about arteriosclerosis, they compare this disease with the plague of the Middle Ages. The question is why are so many people plagued with the buildup of plaque in the arteries? Arteriosclerosis and atherosclerosis are two sides of the same coin. The first one is hardening of the elastic tube, the artery, and filling up these tubes with sludge and blood corpuscles. Atherosclerosis is the fat deposits in and around the arteries, choking the passage of blood and bringing on complete stoppage. The final result of both is a heart attack or a stroke.

HERBAL CHELATION

Herbs, vitamins, minerals and amino acids are a godsend for our health. We can help ourselves by using these important supplements to attain excellent health. They can do wonders for the heart and circulation.

Doctors in Germany recommend hawthorn for people with heart disease. They have learned and applied what herbalists have known for hundreds of years—that hawthorn helps the heart. It is wonderful for problems associated with atherosclerosis, high blood pressure and elevated cholesterol levels. Hawthorn also strengthens heart contractions, lowering blood pressure and lowering pulse rate.

Equisetum arvense is the fancy term for horsetail, which one French medical journal described as having healing properties for the heart. *Equisetum* contains elemental silicon, which is necessary for maintaining flexible arterial walls. As we get older we have less and less silicon and must take *Equisetum* to make up for this loss. When *Equisetum* is combined with hawthorn, the results are amazing. *Equisetum* acts like a broom for the arteries and increases the number of blood corpuscles.

People with heart disease lack chromium and selenium. Our food used to supply us with these minerals but now the soil is losing precious nutrients due to over farming and harsh chemical fertilizers. Animals who graze on selenium depleted soils have weakened heart muscles. Chromium is very important because it improves the ratio of "good" cholesterol to "bad" cholesterol and keeps the overall cholesterol level down. We should consider supplementing with these minerals to avoid complications.

Amino acids can be remarkable for the heart, especially taurine and arginine. Taurine is known to benefit with hardening of the arteries, high blood pressure and even congestive heart failure. This amino acid protects against potassium depletion of the heart, which can lead to seriously irregular heartbeats. Taurine is needed to maintain proper blood platelet functioning. The amino acid arginine is the only source for nitric oxide, which is vital for healthy blood vessels in order to relax the arterial walls so that blood can flow more freely.

Vitamin C helps with blood clotting and high cholesterol levels. It also maintains capillary wall strength. Vitamin C and selenium are important antioxidants for those with heart conditions to protect against stroke.

These items are so divine that they have been referred to as Our Lord's Formula. Aloe vera gel is also recommended to keep circulation flowing.

Take *Herbal Chelation* with 2 tbsp. aloe vera gel before each meal 3 times daily. You can take aloe vera gel alone or put it in apple juice or water but *not* in citrus juices.

Do this for 1 month and then have your physician recheck the health of your arteries. If it is not all gone, repeat. Do not eat heavy meals, potato chips, heavy cakes, alcohol or strong coffee.

In order to keep arteries clear afterwards, consider the French method: 1 kelp tablet and 1 choline tablet (250 mg) 2 times daily.

Yogurt and applesauce is a specific to keep arteries clean.

Reports

"I was scheduled for bypass operation. I knew that only 1 to 4 percent of people die on the operation table, so I was not worried about that and, yet, the closer the scheduled date came, the more nervous I became.

"A friend of mine suggested the cleaning out of the arteries with Our Lord's Formula. First I said, 'Impossible,' but I had nothing to lose, so I started taking Our Lord's Formula with aloe vera gel 3 times daily and also at bedtime. One week went by. I felt better. I could take a deeper breath. I could sleep better. Another week went by and I had no more pressure in my chest. Then I postponed the operation for 2 weeks and after 4 weeks I saw my doctor again. We both could not believe it. The arteries around the heart where they wanted to make the bypass were clear."

Walter Brown, IA

"The pain in my legs was killing me. I could hardly walk 1 or 2 blocks, then I had to rest from pain. My arteries were clogged in the lower extremities. That's what I was told. I went on the Lord's Formula. After only 2 days I found relief. I kept on taking it for 4 weeks and I can walk all I want to without pain."

A. Solari, Denver, CO

"I lost my memory. I could not think of the past or keep my day-times straight. 'Old age,' my daughter said. I misplaced the car keys, I could not remember the TV show, I could not think any longer. A pounding headache came, announcing the inevitable stroke. My daughter found a lady who had taken the Lord's Formula and she brought one month's supply to try it. The month passed. I can think again. First the pounding left. Then my eyes got better and now I can think. I will always treasure this recipe."

Irene Burger

"I had had two chelation therapies and soon needed a third one. I found Our Lord's Formula amazing. I tried it. It worked like a charm. No more trouble."

Eric Warding

"My bypass operation was successful, however, after a year, claudication set in. I limped at times. I had leg pains. I felt tired, exhausted, sleepless. At times my eyes blurred and I was scared. The Lord's Formula worked. No more trouble and it is so easy. No side effects, no pain and no economical disaster—$25 took care of it."

Hilde Bishop, Fort Collins, CO

"My asthma left me after using the Formula for one month."

Anne Myer

SYMPTOMS OF ARTERIOSCLEROSIS

What symptoms does your body give you when plaque is building up in the arteries?

- Watch for an overly tired feeling after a heavy meal.
- Observe forgetfulness with tasks that you normally perform with acuity.
- Notice if your mind will not grasp new ideas or follow new dimensions.
- Persistent feeling of weakness, coldness, tingling or burning in your toes or feet.
- Be aware of dull headaches.
- Persistent sleeplessness is another danger signal.
- Tightness in chest.
- Pain in shoulders when not accident related.
- Breathlessness when walking or lifting.
- Notice if walking gives you pain in the calves of the legs and that, when you rest, you feel better and pain will disappear.
- Notice if you had a good night's sleep. You get up and stretch or exercise. In the middle of the sternum is a sharp pain. It will go away

and not return until the next morning when the same pain returns at the same time in the middle of the sternum.

- Notice if there are small ulcerations of your skin on ankles or feet.
- Notice head noises, dizziness, sudden spells of partial deafness.
- Notice blurred or darkened vision.

SYMPTOMS OF ADVANCED ARTERIOSCLEROSIS

The first signs of plaque buildup in the arteries are not easily recognized. We talked about this already. Symptoms of advanced arteriosclerosis are when the stricken person makes very small steps and has to rest every 100 to 200 yards because of pain in feet and/or legs, particularly calves. Sometimes they limp (it is called claudication) but this is always accompanied with pain. This could be arteriosclerosis in the lower extremities.

Symptoms that may have an underlying cause of blockage in the arteries (a plaque buildup in arteries so that blood and oxygen are not sufficiently supplied to the different organs of the body) are:

- Asthma
- Heart trouble
- High blood pressure
- Loss of memory
- Loss of sleep
- Loss of hearing
- Loss of eyesight
- Leg pain
- Lymph trouble
- Liver trouble
- Kidney trouble
- Diabetes
- Prostate trouble
- Stroke

It sounds harsh, but there is no better prevention and correction of the above disease patterns than the cleaning of your arteries.

When diseased, the venous system can also make pain and give trouble similar to arterial blockage. Here is the difference to observe: When you walk briskly and tightness and pain start in calves and feet and will let up when you stand for a little while, that shows an arterial blockage. In a venous system blockage, pain diminishes as you walk but, when you stand still, pain increases.

WHAT CAUSES ARTERIOSCLEROSIS
AND ATHEROSCLEROSIS?

This is what experts tell us:
- Too much fat intake.
- Too many chemicals in food, water and air.
- Too many metals in food, water and air.
- Too much sodium fluoride buildup.
- Too much sugar (more than 6 tsp. at one time causes blood to coagulate, making tiny blood clots).
- Too much environmental stress.
- Too little exercise.
- Too much smoking.
- Birth control pills.
- Noise pollution is a definite cause of arterial changes.

Kurt Oster, M.D. added that milk cannot be utilized totally unless it is soured, as in yogurt or kefir. His Xanthine Oxidase theory sounds promising. Read Dr. Oster's book. Also read *Fluoride: The Aging Factor* by Dr. John Yiamouyiannis. A fine work of knowledge is presented here.

In 1945, a hospital in Milwaukee designed for mentally disturbed senior citizens was supervised by E. Seiler, M.D., psychiatrist. She ordered all milk removed from the diet. Only yogurt was permitted once a day. Patients had plenty of butter, oils, vegetables, eggs and meats but no milk or ice cream. The results were astounding. After three months the patients became rational and could be taken home. Many of them kept well for years.

TEST YOUR OWN ARTERIAL HEALTH

Foot Test

Walk barefoot for 2 minutes outside in the grass, if possible. Then lie on your back and stretch your legs upwards. Ask someone to look at the soles of your feet. If they show white spots, it indicates that your leg arteries are narrowed down and not enough blood can reach your feet.

Fist Test

1) Lift both hands above your head.
2) Make fists with firm pressure.
3) Open and close fists 10 times.
4) Ask someone to hold your wrists firmly.
5) Open and close again 10 times.
6) Your helper should release the grip on your wrists quickly. In 4 seconds your hands should be really red. If not, you have arterial trouble in your upper torso.

Eye Test

Look in a mirror. Around the colored part of the eye you will find a white ring.

Ear Test

Look at your ear lobes. A crease in the left ear lobe or a star of wrinkles shows arterial trouble around the heart.

WHERE IS THE BLOCKAGE?

You can find out where the blockage is located.

- Pain around hips and the muscle you sit on becoming lame easily may indicate plaque buildup in aorta.
- Pain in thigh may indicate sclerotic buildup in midsection.
- Pain in calves may indicate arterial trouble in arteries leading to legs.
- Pain in feet and toes may indicate a plaque buildup of arteries supplying blood to the feet.

SENECA INDIAN CLEANSING DIET

The Seneca Indians contributed the following diet:

First Day: Eat only fruits and all you want. Try apples, berries, watermelon, pears, peaches, cherries, whole citrus fruits and so forth, but *no bananas.*

Second Day: Drink all the herbal teas you want, such as raspberry, hyssop, chamomile or peppermint. You may sweeten the tea slightly with honey or maple sugar.

Third Day: Eat all the vegetables you want. Have them raw, steamed or both.

Fourth Day: Make a big pot of vegetable broth by boiling cauliflower, cabbage, onion, green pepper, parsley or whatever you have available. Season with sea salt or vegetable broth cubes. Drink only this rich mineral broth all day long.

This diet has the following effect: The first day the colon is cleansed (your wastebasket). The second day you release toxins, salt and excessive calcium deposits in the muscles, tissues and organs. The third day the digestive tract is supplied with healthful, mineral rich bulk. On the fourth day the blood, lymph and inner organs are mineralized. That makes a lot of sense!

YOU NEED ALOE VERA GEL
FOR CLEANSING YOUR ARTERIES

What is aloe vera? Aloe vera is a plant. It has been used for medicinal purposes for centuries. It has been known for its therapeutic advantages and healing properties for more than 4,000 years. Ancient and modern literature abound with references to this unique, natural remedy. It is sometimes called the medicine, miracle or burn plant.

The Greeks, as early as 333 B.C., identified aloe vera as a medicinal herb. The Chinese considered aloe vera sacred and used it for stomach and colon ailments. In the Philippines it is used with milk for dysentery and kidney infections. The Egyptians used it for sunburns and to retard the aging process.

Aloe vera gel aids in assimilation, circulation and elimination. It has been reported to increase endurance and energy and to provide a speedy recovery from fatigue. It has been known to aid in muscle function and utilization of vitamins and minerals. Aloe vera gel assists in achieving healthy skin and hair.

Aloe vera gel is not a drug. It does not react with medications.

Some properties in aloe vera gel:

Active Ingredients	Minerals	Vitamins
Amino acids	Calcium	A
Enzymes	Magnesium	E
Natal aloes	Sodium	K
Aloin	Potassium	B_1
Emodin	Strontium	B_2
Bitter resins	Boron	B_3
Barbaloin	Silicon	B_6
Chlorophyll	Copper	Folic acid
Albumin	Manganese	Choline
Essential oils	Iron	
Gum arabic	Aluminum	
Silica	Lithium	
Phosphate of zinc	Nickel	
	Zinc	

Other agents of aloe vera gel:

- Pain killer
- Fungicidal
- Germicidal
- Virucidal
- Anti-inflammatory: similar to steroid effects
- Antipyretic: reduces fever and heat of sores
- Natural cleanser
- Penetrates tissue
- Dilates capillaries
- Enhances normal cell proliferation: regenerative stage of healing
- Reduces bleeding time

CHOLESTEROL

As already mentioned, arteriosclerosis and atherosclerosis are two sides of the same coin. With atherosclerosis, a fatty, waxy substance clogs arteries inside and out.

The Greek word *athere* means porridge or gruel and the word atherosclerosis is the buildup of a gruel-like substance, called cholesterol, in the blood vessels. "The arteries are so plugged up in some autopsy subjects, that no blood can get through at all," commented a first year medical student.

This abnormal condition with its fatal consequences has caused much controversy over the last 10 years and has been called the plague of modern times. It causes 55 percent of all deaths in the United States and has been the leading cause of death in our country since 1920. Scientists estimate that everyone over the age of 21 suffers to some extent from atherosclerosis and/or arteriosclerosis .

Because of the epidemic proportions that this disease has reached, 20 percent of all research monies spent are used to study it and some interesting findings are being disclosed.

Cholesterol is absolutely essential to the body for the production of bile, for fat absorption in the intestines, for steroid hormone synthesis and as an element in cell membranes. Why do we have trouble with cholesterol buildup when the body needs cholesterol? Atherosclerosis is a complex biochemical problem with no simple answers.

The liver is supposed to make the right amount of cholesterol. A poor liver being overworked and maltreated makes short cuts so that the cholesterol amount is larger and more like glue.

The Truth on Cholesterol

Eskimos are on a high fat, high protein diet. They show very high cholesterol but no arteriosclerosis is found. Their arteries are free of cholesterol buildup. Why?

Cholesterol has two chemicals. LDL, which stands for Low Density Lipoprotein, brings the cholesterol from the liver to the tissue. HDL, which stands for High Density Lipoprotein, removes the excess cholesterol from the tissues and arteries. I call it the "Ajax of the arteries." It is arterial cleansing.

Eskimos have lots of HDL; therefore, their arteries are clean in spite of their high consumption of fats and proteins. (By the way, Eskimos have very efficient kidneys to handle all of the protein they consume.)

A Japanese laboratory found that, in the right shinbone, a special hormone is formed which is picked up by the white corpuscles and delivered to the liver to be utilized for cholesterol processing. Since, in some cases, this hormone is at short supply, cholesterol-triglyceride trouble starts.

Here is an herbal formula that helps to create the missing hormone:

• Okra
• Male fern
• Beth root
• Rhubarb root
• Calamus root

A cup of tea made from arnica and hyssop, 3 times daily, is also helpful.

WHAT CAN BE DONE?

• Please quit your smoking. Nicotine constricts arteries and less blood can circulate through the constricted vessels.
• More walking, more foot exercises.
• Garlic is splendid to make arteries soft and pliable.
• B-complex helps a lot.
• Noise pollution weakens the arteries. Workers subjected to loud music or working under motor noises are prone to high blood pressure and arteriosclerosis.
• Avoid too much salt.
• Avoid too much sugar.
• Choline relaxes the arteries and helps in the fibrillation and irregularity of the heartbeat. Choline is easily counteracted by the enzyme cholinesterase; therefore, it has to be taken frequently. Choline is better assimilated in its natural form and you will find an abundance

of it in wheat germ, malt and grapes. If you combine choline tablets with kelp tablets, cholinesterase cannot counteract choline so easily.

- Bee pollen is a terrific food supplement, especially in regard to supporting your arteries—1/4 tsp. 2 times daily will do.
- Folic acid builds the "Ajax of the Arteries," HDL (High Density Lipoprotein).
- In any case, clean out your arteries with *Herbal Chelation and aloe vera gel.*

PROTECT YOUR ARTERIES

It is important for you to keep your arteries clean. What follows is a simple method that comes from England. It is highly recommended to protect your arteries once a year.

First Day: Grind up 1 almond, place in 1 cup of water and drink.

Second Day: Take 2 almonds, place in 1 cup of water and drink.

Third day, etc.: Take 3 almonds and on and on until you have reached 15 almonds.

Then go down step by step until you are back to 1 almond a day. This also is the best remedy I know to prevent cancer.

DECONGEST YOUR BLOOD

Your blood and platelets form an unwanted glue-like substance. If glue-like substances in the blood are allowed to accumulate, the platelets release a dangerous waste called adenosine diphosphate, or ADP. Once ADP is released, other platelets glue together. They form clumps that obstruct the flow of blood through the vessel and this may lead to blood clots in the heart (heart attack), brain (stroke), lung or other vital organs.

Take some onions and cut them into pieces. Add to water and simmer to make onion water. White and red onions together have more anticlotting power.

Drink 1/2 cup onion water 5 times daily and take 50 mg B6 with each 1/2 cup of onion water. Bananas and tomatoes, rice and millet are allowed.

Do this for 2 days in a row. Then pick up a good healthy diet but continue with vitamin B6. Red clover leaf tea is excellent.

You are as old as your arteries. Old age sets in when arteries are blocked. Old age sets in when parts of your body do not receive enough oxygen or nourishments due to diminished blood supply.

My advice: Clean your arteries with *Herbal Chelation* and aloe vera gel.

DECONGEST YOUR BRONCHIAL TUBES, SINUSES AND LUNGS

Accumulated glue-like sludge can be loosened and eliminated with the following 1- or 2-day diet. Take a glass of warm water, squeeze the juice of ½ to 1 lemon into it, add a little honey and drink this slowly. Make yourself lots of these drinks throughout the day, about 10 glasses, 1 every hour or so.

This will decongest your bronchi, sinuses and lungs. If needed, repeat it every week until all is clear. Do not eat any dry food with it.

CLEANSE YOUR BODY WITH LEMON COCKTAIL

How to make: Juice of ½ lemon to each glass of medium hot or cold water. Add 1 or 2 tbsp. of pure maple syrup or use sorghum or natural molasses that does not contain sulfur dioxide.

45

How to use: Take from 8 to 20 glasses of the cocktail every 24 hours. If at any time you become weak or nervous, you may have 1 glass of strained orange juice during the day but take no other food during the fast.

For those who are overweight, less syrup or molasses may be taken and only about 6 to 8 glasses of the cocktail. An enema, night and morning, is recommended by most doctors for elimination. A cup of laxative herbal tea may be taken at bedtime if needed. 1 tsp. of slippery elm, taken with the cocktail 2 or 3 times during the day, is recommended for an irritated stomach.

Lemon is a loosening and cleansing agent. Its 49 percent potassium level strengthens and energizes the heart, its oxygen builds vitality, its carbon acts as a motor stimulant, its hydrogen activates the sensory nervous system, its calcium strengthens and builds the lungs, its phosphorus knits the bones, its sodium encourages tissue building, its magnesium acts as a blood alkalizer, its iron builds the red corpuscles, its chlorine cleanses the blood plasma and its silicon aids the thyroid for deeper breathing.

The maple syrup or molasses is an eliminator and builder. The natural iron, copper, calcium, carbon and hydrogen help build the blood to normal and give you plenty of energy. It truly is a perfect combination for cleansing, eliminating and healing. 2 days only.

To break the fast: 1 glass of unstrained orange juice may be taken for breakfast in place of the cocktail. A serious mistake is often made when too much food is taken after a fast and much injury to the system is the result. Only light, nourishing food should be taken during the first 2 days after the fast.

DECONGEST YOUR COLON

General Rules for Relieving Constipation

1) First rule: Always drink plenty of pure water!

2) Fresh fruits and vegetables are very important because of roughage. Stewed vegetables and dried fruits are also helpful.

3) Add unprocessed wheat bran and/or unprocessed wheat germ to your daily diet to normalize bowel function!

4) Brewer's yeast is effective for many.

5) Avoid excessive milk drinking.

6) Daily morning or afternoon exercise (yoga, walking in fresh air, etc.).

7) Go to the bathroom daily at the same time after a meal; relax, read there, stay awhile.

8) Reflex massage stimulates the circulation of every gland in the body!

9) Body massage and natural therapy improves circulation, digestion, respiration, organs of elimination and brain and nervous system (receive greater supply of blood).

What Causes a Toxic Colon?
- A toxic colon is caused by eating devitalized food.
- "The American way": Hamburgers, French fries and a malt; macaroni and cheese; and, of course, the big culprit, white bread.
- The walls of the colon are constantly at work absorbing moisture out of the contents of the colon. The longer any material remains in the colon, the more dry and pressed together it becomes, thus becoming gluey, and the glue coats the lining of the colon. This has been proven.
- When autopsies are taken, the lining of the colon is like hardened cement.

Our body is fed through our colon. When the colon is literally poisoned by a cesspool of decayed matter, the toxins released by the putrefactive process get into our bloodstream and travel to all parts of the body. Every cell in the body gets affected and many forms of sickness can result. It weakens the entire system. A toxic colon can be the causative factor for nearly any disease.

Illnesses due to toxic colons (asthma, hay fever, arteriosclerosis, cancer, arthritis, neuritis, hypertension, diabetes, etc.) are just manifestations of toxins that should escape through the lymphatic system. But, due to the overload, they are unable to so mucoid substance settles in the lungs, muscles, tendons and joints.

If a toxic colon is the underlying cause of many diseases, it makes sense that it should be our first choice in helping ourselves to clean and decongest our colon.

Because we are fed through the colon, this is where health and disease are determined. If a person has a toxic colon, all the good food and vitamins will have to pass through this toxic colon, thus lessening their nutritional value and polluting the body. The blood is only as clean as the intestinal tract because it absorbs both nutritive and toxic materials from the colon.

Here are several methods to cleanse your colon:

- Earl Irons method: Bentonite clay and cleanser for 7 days.
- An herbal combination of yellow dock, onion, sage, wahoo bark and rhubarb root.
- An herbal combination of white pine bark, mugwort, myrrh, chamomile, catnip and mullein.
- 1 tbsp. glycerin in 1 cup of coffee.
- 1 qt lightly salted water upon rising.

DECONGEST YOUR BOWELS WITH FLAX SEED

Flax seed must be gently simmered for, say, ½ hour and then allowed to stand where it will remain hot for 1 to 2 hours. Put 2 tbsp. in 2 cups of boiling water; let it boil down to 1 cup. Add a little sugar to taste. The juice of ½ lemon makes a tasty addition. Drink the whole cupful at bedtime and swallow all the seeds. The mucilage is soothing to the bowels and, in combination with the seeds, often produces a good bowel movement. This combination is excellent to take about once a week or every 4 days or more often if needed, as it is harmless.

MUCOUS CLEANSER

This diet to clear mucous out of intestines was donated to this book by a chiropractor in Los Angeles. It is amazing to see the amount of mucous leaving the body in people who you never suspected had this trouble.

Buy:
- Unfiltered apple juice
- Psyllium seeds, Mucovada, Intesto-Klez or ground flax seeds

- Papaya tablets
- Pancreatin
- Comfrey and pepsin
- Fenugreek seed

Schedule:

7 A.M.

1 glass distilled water with 1 tsp. bulk (mentioned above)
apple juice with papaya tablet
1 pancreatin
1 comfrey and pepsin
1 cup fenugreek seed tea

Do this every 2 hours until 9 P.M. and keep it up for 3 to 4 days. All mucous is cleansed, even from sinuses.

HIGH FIBER DIET

The main function of fiber in a diet is to normalize the transit of food through the digestive system, allowing efficient elimination of waste matter. To quote one author, "We've been around for 3½ million years thriving on a high fiber diet for all but the last 50 years. And this is beginning to show with dramatic increases in a wide variety of diseases, from heart disease to colon cancer . . ." including the diverticular diseases—hemorrhoids, appendicitis, ulcerative colitis and constipation. Physicians are finding that when more fiber rich food is eaten, these diseases tend to disappear.

Dr. Andrew Stanway, former chief physician at King's College Hospital in London and a nutrition expert, explains one reason why: "The swift movement of bran (and other fibers) through the body means that cancer causing agents have less time to start the processes leading to colon cancer. This fast movement also prevents conditions such as gallstones, stomach ailments and circulatory problems."

Dr. Siegal, author of *Dr. Siegal's Natural Fiber Permanent Weight-Loss Diet* and whose clinics have successfully used a high fiber diet with 5,000 patients last year, says that "a high bran diet with few refined carbohydrates will safely take pounds off and keep them off."

Dr. Emanuel Cheraskin of the University of Alabama Dental School and author of 13 books on the relationship between diet and disease, says a high fiber diet will help prevent heart disease, colon cancer, gallstones, stomach ailments, hemorrhoids and blood clots.

When we think of fiber food, we think of bran. Yes, it is the richest food in fiber, however, it has a drawback. The sharp edges of the bran may injure the already sick colon. Please add wheat germ to your bran. Wheat germ is also high in fiber and has some health giving, vitamin E rich oils in it which lubricate the bran. Then the danger of bran bulking in the intestines is over.

Raw and cooked vegetables, whole grain breads, fruit, berries, beans and corn all have fibers and will keep a healthy colon at its best. Once a colon is sick, weakened or diseased, special care and diets have to be utilized.

I summarize: Recent findings tell us that fiber "is the important thing." Formerly we were told not to use fiber as it might cause a variety of colon troubles. Where is the truth?

The truth is in the wholeness of food. The carrot has fiber, the whole potato has it, the grains have bran and, hidden in this natural fiber, are minerals which we will not get if we eat only a part from the wholeness.

Imagine:

- Protein drink for breakfast.
- Donut and coffee between telephoning.
- Soft bread and soft cheese for lunch.
- A small salad for supper with mashed potatoes and meat.
- Cakes and cookies on top.

Just not enough fiber!

Bran, a natural food fiber, is tasteless and easy to take. Mix 3 tbsp. bran and 3 tbsp. raw or toasted wheat germ. "You just add it to any kind of food you want, from soup to cereals to ground beef."

DECONGEST YOUR JOINTS: ARTHRITIS

When arthritis sets in one must adjust the *lifestyle*. You turn to ½ cooked and ½ raw diet. Leave out sugar, cakes, cookies, potato chips and heavy meals.

Start exercising by swinging arms and legs. Bend your knees, twist and stretch your body.

Infection . . . Dr. Douglas Backer from England brought the news to America that most arthritis, osteoarthritis and rheumatism have a hidden virus. In England they found that a dog virus is responsible for these pains. In this country the herbal antidote is a combination of yucca, black walnut leaves, yellow dock, wormwood and fenugreek seed. This is used to straighten out the damage.

Four different foods are most advantageous. Dale Alexander speaks about cod-liver oil. Buy his book for your own information. One tbsp. cod-liver oil in orange juice at bedtime. One tbsp. almond oil in cherry juice upon rising. You can also use safflower oil or peanut oil. Five to 7 alfalfa juice tablets with each meal. Alfalfa releases the stiffness in joints and muscles. Two glasses cherry juice or a saucer full of cherries a day. This counteracts uric acid.

To rebuild the undernourished adrenal gland, which is so significant in arthritis, take licorice root, stress B with C, pantothenic acid and extra B_{12} and B_6 when the hands are affected. This will make your adrenal gland produce its own cortisone and other hormones. Omit coffee and sugar.

Be sure that you take calcium with magnesium. It is a tranquilizer, a builder, a pain reliever and an absolute must in all kinds of arthritic suffering.

- 2 parts calcium
- 1 part magnesium

Take ½ of your calcium-magnesium intake with cod-liver oil.

DECONGEST YOUR GALLBLADDER:
APPLE JUICE DIET

I have a book from the 17th century in which an old physician from Austria gives his secrets. One of them is the apple juice diet. This diet is greatly used among health minded people to detoxify liver and gallbladder. Here is one report: "I had had a very bad summer. Too much work, too little sleep. I did not take food supplements and had to work under conditions where I had to eat fried foods and other no-no foods. In the fall it started. Tired, bloated, listless, I caught myself being sarcastic and nasty. One night I had terrible pain over my right shoulder and neck. I am sorry to say my liver quit her job and the next morning I went on the apple juice diet. The bright green pebbles, the old bile, just poured out on the third day and I was myself again."

Here it is and I very, very highly recommend it to everyone. Give your gallbladder a rest, a chance, a holiday.

First Day:

8 A.M.	1 glass (8 oz)	apple juice
10 A.M.	2 glasses (16 oz)	apple juice
12 P.M.	2 glasses (16 oz)	apple juice
2 P.M.	2 glasses (16 oz)	apple juice
4 P.M.	2 glasses (16 oz)	apple juice
6 P.M.	2 glasses (16 oz)	apple juice

Juice should be natural, without chemicals. No food is to be taken this day.

Second Day:

Same procedure as the first day. No food this day either. At bedtime take 4 oz olive oil. You may wash the olive oil down with hot lemon juice or hot apple juice. Go to bet at once.

As a rule this diet starts to work around 4 A.M. In the fecal matter you will find little green pebbles. They may be the size of a pinhead or they may be as big as a bird egg. Many times it all looks like green mud.

In any case, the old stagnant bile becomes dissolved and liquefied through the malic acid of the apple juice—which should be sugar and chemical free —and the oil moves the whole mess.

Dr. Adolphus Hohensee had been using this diet on thousands of his students all over America. In Europe it is practiced in health spas and hospitals with equal results. It re-establishes the normal function of the liver. This diet "frees the liver-gallbladder tract from old bile and debris, which we call stones!"

52

DECONGEST YOUR EYES: GLAUCOMA

What follows is a 3-month program which entails a very low carbohydrate diet and no sugar or coffee (or very, very weak coffee).

First month:

100,000 IU vitamin A once daily (½ from beta carotene and ½ from fish oil).

20 mg B-complex before each meal.

25 mg B_2 before each meal.

Coffee enema once daily.

Chop a large onion once daily so you can have a good cry.

Second month:

75,000 IU vitamin A (½ from beta carotene and ½ from fish oil).

No coffee enema.

The rest as mentioned in the first month.

Third month:

50,000 IU vitamin A (½ from beta carotene and ½ from fish oil).

The rest is the same as the second month.

To combat congestion of eyes, take juices of ½ potato, ½ cucumber, ½ onion and ¼ pepper. Drink 6 oz of this ½ hour before supper and watch your eyes get cleaner after 30 days.

DECONGEST YOUR KIDNEYS

A great deal of attention should be placed on the kidneys. A sick kidney does not hurt until the sickness expands to the outer encasing. Then it hurts badly, especially when stones are passing through the kidney ducts.

A sick kidney presses upwards. It gives a stiff neck, disk trouble, stiff and painful arms, back troubles and fuzzy eyesight.

In advanced cases, kidney troubles express in sore knees and, finally, swollen ankles.

Two-thirds of all people committed to mental institutions have kidney disorders. Some get wild or disoriented and then the kidney should be checked.

The right kidney is the organ to filter inorganic substances, such as toxic lead, mercury, copper, DDT and arsenic bound chemicals. When overloaded, this organ does not hurt but becomes cold to the touch (you feel it cold).

The left kidney is sensitive to infections.

For cleansing the kidneys take an 8 oz glass of raw beet juice, taking 1 tsp. at a time all day long, making the 8 oz last the whole day, with nothing eaten that day. The urine turns red as the system absorbs the beet juice drop by drop. A day of this every 6 months is truly a food used as a medicine. Water allowed.

DECONGEST YOUR KIDNEYS FROM STONES

Because of your interest and concern about kidney stones, I am acquainting you with Dr. Christian Chaussy's kidney stone research.

Dr. Chaussy, a compassionate German research urologist, gave a paper to the American Urological Association in Boston, reporting on 72 kidney stone cases in which he and his group had successfully pulverized the stones extracorporeally, without resorting to surgery. Unfortunately, we have been unable to find any place in the USA where stones from high in the ureter can be removed safely without surgery.

Small wonder that Dr. Chaussy's research facility, which is subsidized by grants from the German government, cannot begin to accept all of the patients from around the world who write asking to be accepted into his program. Dr. Chaussy does on occasion, however, take patients from other countries. His grant covers work only on stones in the kidney, not in the ureter.

It is important to drink plenty of fluids, especially in warm weather, if you ever have had or think you might have a tendency to form kidney stones. Adults should drink enough to produce 2 to 2½ liters of urine every day. (Measure your output—about 5 pints (10 cups)—until you are sure your intake is sufficient to assure this large volume of urine.)

The American Journal of Medicine, Volume 71, October 1981, said, "The efficacy of thiazide and allopurinol in the prevention of calcium stones has long been established in large series of patients with renal calculi (1-3). However, at the customary dosage of hydrochlorothiazide, 50 mg twice a day, the incidence of side effects (such as hypokalemia, extracellular volume depletion, hyperuricemia, weakness, fatigue and mental irritability) may necessitate discontinuation of treatment in a significant proportion (10 to 35 percent) of patients (1, 4)."

For kidney stones take 7 oz dark grape juice and add ½ tsp. cream of tartar. Take 2 oz 3 times daily before meals and drink 1 qt of the following tea daily and keep it up for 5 weeks: Equal parts knotgrass and chamomile. Drink a little all day long and do not ice it!

STONE AND GOUT REMEDY

1 qt apple cider
1 tsp. hydrangea root

Let these stand for 12 hours, bring to a boil, simmer and drink ½ cup 3 times daily. Also take 15 to 20 sour cherries every morning for 3 weeks.

DECONGEST YOUR LYMPHATIC SYSTEM

Recipe:

1 pt. white grapefruit juice
1 pt. freshly squeezed orange juice
1 pt. grape juice
1 pt. water with the juice of 3 limes
1 pt. water with the juice of 2 lemons
1 pt. frozen pineapple juice, diluted
1 pt. papaya juice, diluted
12 whole eggs
6 egg yolks
Frozen raspberries or strawberries add a delicious flavor
Beat eggs and mix into fruit juice mixture

This is 1 day's supply. If you are hungry add 1 kind of fresh fruit. For lunch, green salad and/or sprouts with raw almond dressing. For supper, green salad and/or sprouts with raw almond dressing and 1 steamed vegetable.

Recipe:

Drink 4 to 5 cups of cucumber juice daily for 1 week. It purifies the lymphatic system and the blood and clears the complexion.

Recipe:

Boil 3 tbsp. barley in 1 qt water for 30 minutes. Add a little clove and cinnamon. Drink this in 1 day. It will clear the congestion in the lymphatic system.

Recipe:

1 pt. apple juice or apple wine

1 pt. water

1 pt. milk

Heat slowly and do not bring to a boil. When it curdles, strain it through a fine cloth, throw curds away and sweeten with honey if needed. Take 2 tbsp. 5 times daily if person is very weak. Appetite will come soon. As patient gets stronger, give up to 2 cups daily. It is powerful.

NERVES

It takes will power and authority to stay on a diet, especially when your nerves give out.

3 Days for Better Nerves:

The following routine, only 3 days in a row, will make a better "boss," a stronger personality out of you. After that, 1 day a week or 1 day every 2 weeks will keep your nerves sweet.

In 1 pint of cottage cheese mix 3 tbsp. almond oil or safflower oil and 2 egg yolks. Mix well and either make it sweet with honey or spicy with onions, salt and herbs. Also boil 4 tbsp. of barley in 2 qt of water for 35 minutes. Strain and add honey or lime or lemon juice to the barley water so it tastes good.

Before breakfast:	1 cup of warm barley water
Breakfast:	Prepared cottage cheese and carrots, raw or cooked
Mid-morning:	Barley water

Noon:	Steamed zucchini, cooked green beans and cottage cheese (spicy)
Mid-afternoon:	Barley water
Evening:	Prepared cottage cheese, zucchini (stewed or baked in the oven), dish of barley, carrot salad and barley water
Bedtime:	Barley water and calcium tablets

PREGNANCY

Dr. V. Noodan estimated that the needed caloric intake of a fetus during pregnancy between the second and fifth months is 150 calories and, later on, 300 to 400 calories over the needs of the mother. That is not very much. However, the quality of the food is important.

While speaking of quality we think of proteins but, in pregnancy, this is not the way to go. The unborn needs minerals, such as calcium, iron, magnesium, zinc and the whole row of trace minerals, organic and inorganic. For instance, it was calculated that the fetus needs 34 g of pure calcium to develop properly.

If there is not enough calcium, the new developing body will rob it from the mother.

If during pregnancy a mother refrains from salt, she can drink all the fluids she wants without causing edema.

The following recipe has helped many from pregnancy intoxications: 1 level tsp. Epsom salts in 6 oz water every hour, 4 times. That will relieve the danger at once.

Whenever albumin shows in the urine of the mother, *no* milk should be given any longer. Diluted fruit juices, water and vegetable juices are to be taken.

The normal development of the child is dependent on the presence of enough vitamins, such as A, B-complex, C-complex, E and D. One hundred IU of vitamin E is a must. Vitamin A is best through carrots.

Therefore, in the state of pregnancy, every woman should have vitamin and mineral supplements, good natural foods, vegetables and fruits and whole grains. A natural food diet is the best assurance against miscarriages and gives a happy pregnancy.

57

PHLEBITIS

- Eat sparingly.
- Drink plenty of diluted fruit or vegetable juices—6 oz juice to 2 oz water.
- No meat, cheese or egg allowed.
- Make a tea of: 2 parts white oak bark, 1½ parts St. John's wort and 2 parts yarrow. Drink 1 qt cool tea daily and also apply cool tea to the leg.
- Drink 6 oz aloe vera juice over the course of 1 day and eat 2 tbsp. blackstrap molasses daily.
- An extra good fruit juice combination for phlebitis is:

> 2 tbsp. maple syrup
> 1 glass water
> Dash of red root or paprika
> Drink ½ glass every hour for 1 day or more

DECONGEST YOUR LIVER

The liver is the most affected organ when it comes to metal and chemical poisoning. You have to clean out your liver—old debris, metals (such as lead, mercury, arsenic), chemicals (such as DDT) and so on.

Every time that you have the following symptoms, a liver flush is indicated:

- When you start to ache without reason.
- When you touch your right collarbone on the knob and it is painful to touch.
- When you become disenchanted with life.
- When you find fault with your neighbor.
- When you are comfortable with dark glasses.

Then it is time to clean your liver. Buy large cans of stewed tomatoes. Better to make your own but do not add any fat. Eat as much as you can and also drink tomato juice.

It is amazing how hungry you become, so at bedtime of the second day you will look forward to the following cocktail:

3 oz olive oil
2 oz castor oil
3 oz whip cream

Stir and drink this before bed when you are ready for sleep and relaxed. You may chew a little piece of lemon afterwards just for taste. It is a lot easier than it sounds. At 3 or 4 A.M. you will be having a nature' s call and, in all your life, you have not experienced so much dark and ugly smelling waste. The next morning have a breakfast you desire and earned.

Accumulation of toxins in the body may occur due to failure of the detoxification systems—liver, kidney, thyroid, adrenals and colon. Accumulation may also be due to faulty metabolism or toxic matter at large.

DECONGEST YOUR LIVER AND PANCREAS

Soak 1 lb. dried apricots in pineapple juice overnight. Next morning blend it and add fresh pineapple pieces and juice so that it becomes thick enough to spoon it. Divide it into 4 portions and eat it morning, noon, night and bedtime, preferably not eating anything else that day. *Do not use if you are a diabetic.*

DECONGEST YOUR SPLEEN

The spleen is the reservoir to store electricity in the body. If the spleen is not in ordcer, the brain takes over this job. However, it has one drawback. People become egocentric. They accomplish nothing worthwhile.

Okra and red beeds are revitalizing foods for the spleen.

Recipe:
2 qt concord grape juice
Juice of 6 oranges
Juice of 3 lemons

Cut the white of the lemon into small pieces. Boil this in a little water for 10 minutes. Add water to the drink. Then take distilled water and fill the liquid mixture to 1 gallon. This is 1 day's supply of your food-drink intake. Just 2 days of this will cleanse your organs as Drano cleanses your water pipes.

DECONGEST YOUR SKIN

Tissue Cleansing:

Make yourself 6 oz of fresh orange juice 10 times daily. Add 2 oz of distilled water and drink slowly. Drink a hot tea made from wood sanicle and peppermint 3 times daily, that is, morning, noon and night. No food.

After 2 to 3 days, your skin will be different. The calcium deposits in your body will be lessened due to the lime in the oranges. You may continue the orange juice another 3 days but eat apples, pears, berries and cottage cheese.

DECONGEST YOUR STOMACH

"A sick stomach makes crippled, stiff hands."

The following foods are particularly healing to sick stomachs—to ulcers, pain, discomfort and sufferings from stomach distress.

- Carrot
- Coconut milk
- Eggplant
- Flax seed tea
- Slippery elm tea with cream
- Goat's milk
- Okra
- Egg white
- Parsnip
- Sweet potato
- Cottage cheese
- Aloe vera juice, best of all

No grapefruit for stomach troubled people.

If you are anxious to be healed from stomach ulcers, try the carrot diet. Boil a good quantity of carrots in pure water, such as artesian. Avoid aluminum of any kind, whether found in pots, pans or foil. After the carrots are done, try them in various ways. Take a napkin and eat them rabbit style. Mash them or puree them. Boil them after they are cooked or make a soup with them. Slice them lengthwise or in squares. No butter or salt may be added. This is all you eat for 7 days. Twice daily you may have 6 oz of raw carrot juice, either with cream (2 tbsp.) or with goat's milk (6 oz).

DECONGEST YOUR STOMACH FROM MUCOUS

Mucous cleansers of the stomach are taken in the following manner: 1 glass fresh orange juice, same amount of distilled water. Do not mix. First drink the orange juice, then follow with the water. Do this as often as you want, 10 times daily or so. No other food should be taken. Do it 2 days in a row 2 to 3 times a year.

ELECTROMAGNETISM

We do not only have the physical body to care for but the electro-magnetic body has to be healed also. We have several methods to do that.

- Touch for Health
- Reiki
- Structural Integration
- Acupuncture
- The Laying on of Hands

History

The "laying on of hands" is as old as mankind itself. Why then did it come to so much discredit when the Cabala teaches it in detail and the Indians used it in their "Veda system of healing." The primitives used it and the king of all kings, Jesus Christ, used it. Furthermore, Jesus said, "This and more thou shall do in my name." And what follows is how it happened.

In the Middle Ages the "laying on of hands" was mainly practiced by the kings and rulers. It was a "royal art." Edward III, for example, was considered a supersaint. He reportedly healed 136 people in one afternoon session.

Frederick Barbarossa was a healing king. Charlemagne was called a saint because of the many healings which took place under his hands.

The House of the Habsburgs had many fine healing kings. Maximilian, who died in the year 1519, had such outstanding healing qualities that many celebrities of other countries came to pay him a visit in order to be healed.

The House of Burgundy (France) likewise had outstanding healing kings. They were called "Sons of God's Grace." One of the best known healers was Charles X. He reportedly healed 128 people in one afternoon with the famous phrase, "The King touches you and God heals you." Philip I was very successful in healing scrofula, which, as we know it now, is a deficiency disease.

61

Basically, the kings touched the forehead of their subjects and made the sign of the cross. Many times they used holy water which was made by themselves.

The ritual for making holy water was a secret and it was handed down from father to son, from ruler to ruler, from generation to generation and, finally, holy water was partially adopted by the churches.

At that time there used to be no conflict between the ruling kings and the medics. Every royal family had medics employed. The healing by a king was not a cure-all. It was considered an act of God performed through the hands of the king.

Introduction

Man has constantly been searching the universe for a simple, better way to regain and maintain better health. We have long been aware that our bodies have both a positive side and a negative side. There has been much written on this.

We have polarity and magnetic healing. Both use the negative and the positive but neither opens the flow of electromagnetic power to the organs. The head is the control tower and the neck is the magnetic keyboard to the entire body.

In our Aquarian Age it is only natural that we should turn to the electromagnetic forces to find our answers, to obtain perfect health (Mildred Konsella).

Magnetism is a natural energy. Our earth in itself is a giant magnet with positive and negative poles. Forces released by the magnetic North Pole encircle our earth and, as we know, the energies affect all living things. We are bathed in this electromagnetic force field and no life would exist without it. Scientists tell us that, basically, magnetism is generated in the atoms. That means that we also are magnets in our own rights.

We are magnetic generators. We live on top of a magnet in the influence of magnetic energies of other planets and worlds and we still know very little about this subject. Einstein said, "The knowledge about that which we know is only a fraction from that which we do not know." In fact, when it comes to the healing arts and magnetism this subject is called "dark force," "witchcraft" or "special gift" and its results are called "unbelievable" or "unreal." It is condemned and ridiculed and still it has remained with us since mankind has existed. Mankind did not know why this laying on of hands helped but now, with the help of many scientists, we know and this book is a guideline for every woman and man who is willing to help his fellow man. Remember Jesus Christ said, "This and more thou shall do in my name." Do it in the name of the Most High!

Healing with magnetism is the oldest form of healing known to mankind. The Cabala teaches it. The old Hindu healing system taught it. It was taught in the mystery schools of the Orient and Occident and in every mother is the original urge to place her hand over her youngster's feverish forehead, aching back or sore thumb.

We are very much inclined to call it suggestive healing but there is more to it than suggestion. Goethe said: "Magnetism is an all-present, all-reaching power. Every human being has it. Only according to the human individuality it differs in strength. Its action works on everything and magnetism is everywhere." We do not have to doubt any longer that a power leaves our hands. The Kirlian photography shows and proves that.

The electromagnetic force field is *not* the only energy which can be employed and used for healing. There is the prana energy, an energy which penetrates each cell of our body and flows from East to West. There also is the so-called sun-moon energy which is expressed in certain Christ-close people and this is a gift of the Divine to which I know only one fitting key. It is to work on the development of your light within you. When path and goal are one, this power will develop.

To make sure you understand this book, it is a textbook for the "laying on of hands" which makes use of the tremendous electromagnetic power of the universe.

The entire body of man is a field of flowing electromagnetic energy. Wherever this flow stops, for one reason or another, we have a short circuit and the pattern of life and health is impaired.

The laying on of hands in the right manner may aid in bringing back the energy to full flow and repair the short circuit. Before we go into details one has to know the exact manner and flow of the human biomagnetic energies.

MAGNETO THERAPY: THE LAYING ON OF HANDS

In front the right side is positive, the left side is negative (Fig. 1). Please observe that the magnetic poles in the human body are just below the navel. There it is neutral. Over the sex organs there is a strong positive biomagnetic field.

We had had the erroneous concept that the spine is the neutral point, the magnetic pole, but, digging into the knowledge of the Cabala, I found that the ancients knew differently and by measuring these points I found it is true. This knowledge is of great significance and the laying on of hands becomes a science of great importance.

The backside is more complicated. Note in Fig. 2 that the back of the head has a strong positive biomagnetic field. Also, the base of the spine is strongly positive. In between these two positive poles the spine is negatively charged. The right kidney is positive. The left kidney is negative. The right shoulder plate is positive. The left shoulder plate is negative. The right hip is positive. The left hip is negative.

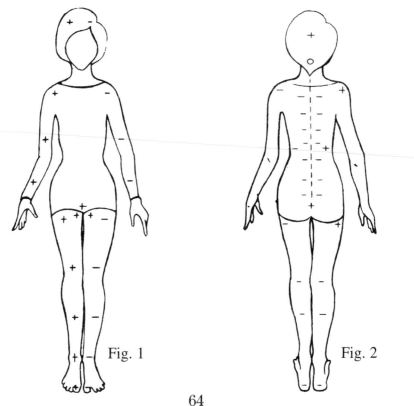

Fig. 1   Fig. 2

In order to have results we have to turn our full attention to our work. With every stroke, with every movement, we should realize the healing power of the Divine.

Realize that you are able to increase the result of your work by increasing the power of your mind to which there is no limitation. A concentrated thought pattern releases energies which become vital and necessary for magneto therapy. Do not undress anyone. You have to release the anxiety and not increase it by embarrassment.

In acute cases and in nervous disorders always reduce the electromagnetic activity with the soothing power of the left hand. In all healing crises which may occur, again work with the left hand and give support to the magnetic pole with the right hand.

The duration of the treatment is between 5 and 10 minutes. In acute cases you want to do it every day. In others once a week.

Magneto therapy is nothing new. It has been used since mankind has existed. New is the understanding of the electromagnetic poles and the proper placement of the hands. New also is the understanding of positive and negative ions. New are discoveries of electromagnetic functioning of the very cells of the different parts of the body—the blood as an electromagnetic stream of power, the nervous system as the tract for speedy delivery of electromagnetic impulses. All this knowledge is new and exciting.

Magneto therapy is not meant to replace and will not take away your need for a physician, a surgeon or a hospital. It is not meant to replace and will not eliminate the need for a proper diet or medicine. It is not a replacement for the need for vitamins or minerals but it will increase the ability to live in a poisoned world more efficiently. It will bring into balance the delicate electromagnetic system. Without this we cannot exist.

There are times when it is needed as an emergency and, always and in all cases, the treatments only help to complement the work of your physician.

Magneto therapy can never injure or hurt but only strengthen the healing process which takes place in every organism. Remember, no one heals but God and nature. Every healing attempt is only a little help to the healing process taking place through the power of the Divine.

Magneto therapy always influences the whole body. Children often-times are restless, nervous, lacking in energy, moody or fearful. The cause may be a malfunctioning organ, lack of a certain nutrient or intoxication by heavy metals. Your physician will find the cause. An electromagnetic treatment in all cases will harmonize the nervous system and the organs. God is law and order and when we follow these laws of guiding, directing and organizing the unorderly, distorted, electromagnetic body of the sick to the order of the universe, health is on its way.

There are three fundamental stroke patterns, three distinct movements.

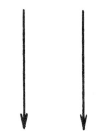

Fig. 3   The Parallel Stroke or Straight Stroke

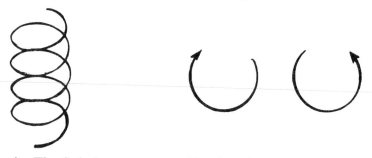

Fig. 4   The Spiral   Fig. 5   The Circle or Loop

The parallel stroke or straight stroke movement influences mainly the entire digestive tract. The spiral movement influences mostly the nervous system. The circle movement is not closed but is an open loop. It is for heart, lungs and congested areas.

No part of the body is active unless magnetic energy flows to it. This flow of magnetic energy is the basic principle of magnetic healing.

A schooled magneto therapist is capable of relieving conditions of pain and discomfort and only 1 or 2 treatments are needed. Your hands must be dry. No magnetic flow can take place when your hands are wet. Rub your hands together until they are hot. Then place the fingertips of your right hand in the palm of your left hand. Raise to your toes and will for the electromagnetic powers to go through you and over you for helping and energizing purposes of your fellow man. This takes only 45 to 60 seconds. Then your body is turned into the magnetic flow.

Always keep your mind positive. Imagine perfect health and realize that you become a tool for the powers of the universe and a servant to the Lord. A great help was given to me by Dr. Doreal. He said to imagine the flow of magnetism increasing and flowing very rapidly. I learned to increase the flow of electromagnetism by imagination. I see a little brook, a small amount of water trickles down and, as I hold my hands, I imagine the increase of water in the brook until it is in complete and mighty flow unobstructed by stones or branches. Washing away obstacles of all kinds is the idea.

The Parallel Stroke or Straight Stroke

To work with the biomagnetic forces please do not undress your patient. Let him take off his shoes and make his feet feel comfortable. A well padded massage table is best. A couch or a mat on the floor will do.

Stand on the right side of your friend and tell him to close his eyes and to concentrate on the light within, the healing power of Christ within or the electromagnetic power of the universe. Tell him or her that they are a child of the universe, subject to the universal laws and powers.

Remember your right hand is positive so it has to stroke the left side of your friends' body. The left hand is negative so it will stroke the right side. The strokes have to be very light in nature, slow in character, thumbs 2 inches apart. You start from head down but leave the crown of the head untouched (Fig. 6). Go particularly slow over trouble areas like the liver and intestines. Concentrate intensely on your work and realize and feel the balance you are bringing back.

When you arrive at the hips you swing out, shake your hands and in a wide movement draw your hands back to the head. (Shaking of hands and the wide semicircle is needed to break the magnetic current.) Never let your hands glide back over the body to the head. You would undo with a single stroke all the strokes previously done.

67

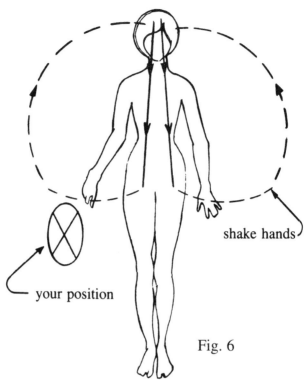

shake hands

your position

Fig. 6

Keep it up for 3 to 4 minutes. This procedure is fundamental in all magneto therapy movements. They should always be the first strokes you do. It normalizes and harmonizes the digestive tract and balances all electromagnetic functions in general.

If you want to stimulate the body take the right hand only. The right hand adds fire to the magnetic system.

Place your left hand on top of your friend (Fig. 7). Stroke with the right hand from head to toe. For a tall person you have to let him flex the knees so you can reach the toes without taking your hand off the head. The stroke has to go clear off the toes. Shake your hand and in a wide semicircle bring it back up to the head.

The Spiral

With the spiral movement we influence the entire nervous system. Have your friend lying comfortably on your well padded massage table. Again do not have clothes removed. Only the shoes and heavy coats are

68

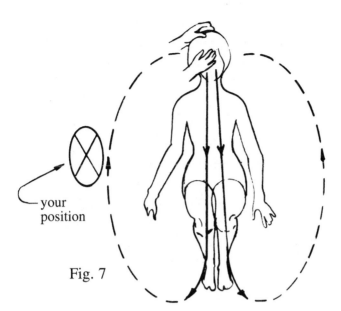

your
position

Fig. 7

removed. You are not giving a Swedish massage. You are dealing with higher powers and we know they penetrate the material covering of your spirit's vehicle, your body.

In case you need a stimulating effect, as in a depressed state or when feeling low vitality in general, place your left hand over the head with your right hand performing clockwise spiral motions over body from head to toe. The spiral has to have the circumference of the width of the body. (Fig. 8.)

Having arrived at the toes, shake your hand and with a wide swing come back to the head and perform this movement for 3 to 5 minutes.

The calming effect will be achieved by placing the right hand

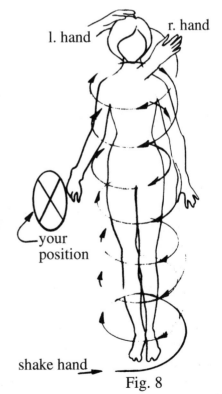

l. hand

r. hand

your
position

shake hand

Fig. 8

69

over the toes (point fingers in the direction of the toes). The left hand performs counterclockwise spirals from head over the toes. Shake your hands and in a wide semicircle come back to the top of the head.

The Circle

The third movement is the circle. This movement is a little open loop. It is a small movement not larger than a silver dollar.

The counterclockwise circle is performed with your left hand and is soothing and calming. The clockwise circle is performed with your right hand and is stimulating. The duration of the circular movement should be 1 to 2 minutes, never longer. This technique is used after you used the first and/or the second technique—the straight stroke and/or the spiral stroke.

It is mainly used for bringing heart, lung, liver and circulation into balance and harmony. It is also used to close energy leakages and to open congestion of various kinds.

How is it done?

DECONGESTION AND STIMULATION
WITH MAGNETO THERAPY

Stimulation of Heart

In case you want to stimulate the heart, place your left hand on top of your friend's head. With the right hand perform 70 small, open, clockwise loops per minute. You can also do this to yourself. Start at the left side of your head, come down doing the loop, over the neck, over the entire sternum around the heart and, after the seventieth stroke, shake your hand. Go back to the starting point and do it once more. (Fig. 9.)

These little, open circles or loops must be feather weight in touch and the sicker the person, the lighter the stroke must be. In severe cases you hardly touch the body and perform another "loop treatment." Use a less firmer stroke 2 hours later.

In case you want to calm the heartbeat place your right hand on your friend's knees (drawn up) and perform 70 loops per minute with your left hand, counterclockwise in the same manner as described before.

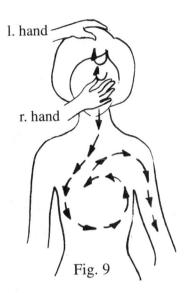

l. hand

r. hand

Fig. 9

Stimulation of Breathing

In case you want to stimulate the lungs and breathing, follow as indicated. Again place your left hand on top of your own or your friend's head. With your right hand start at the right side in clockwise movements of 18 circles per minute, come down the side of the neck, over the right shoulder, cover the entire chest and return to the starting point. Repeat once more. (Fig. 10.)

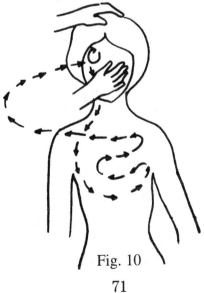

Fig. 10

Soothing-Calming

For a calming effect place your right hand on the toes of your friend. Point fingers in the direction of the toes. The left hand makes the strokes from head over the toes. Shake your hands and in a wide semicircle come back to the top of the head.

Another way is to place your right hand on the drawn up knees of your friend and with the left hand perform the circle movement in a counterclockwise loop.

Decongest Your Gallbladder

The small circle method is used to open up congested areas. An example is a blocked up gallbladder. Do this 18 times clockwise with the right hand. For an infected gallbladder, 18 times counterclockwise with the left hand.

Constipation

Right hand clockwise 70 times per minute. Follow large intestine with left hand on top of head. (Fig. 11.)

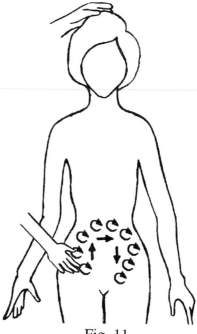

Fig. 11

72

Stimulation of Circulation

To stimulate circulation place left hand on top of stomach, finger pointing down. With your right hand stroke left leg with parallel strokes from the groin, down over the left leg, over foot. Interrupt the magnetic lock by shaking hand and in a wide semicircle start at the groin down. Alternate the hands for 5 minutes. Perform the open loop technique clockwise on both sides of groin for 1 minute. In case of varicose veins in addition to this, apply the open loop technique counterclockwise on the bend of the foot.

Itching

When people itch all over, the following magnetic treatment is of great value: Brush body from head to toe with your hands spread out and thumbs touching each other.

- Front 7 times
- Back 7 times
- Right arm 7 times
- Left arm 7 times

Bringing the Body into Balance

Fig. 12 shows an excellent method for bringing the body back into balance. Lightly stroke the head and spine as shown in the diagram.

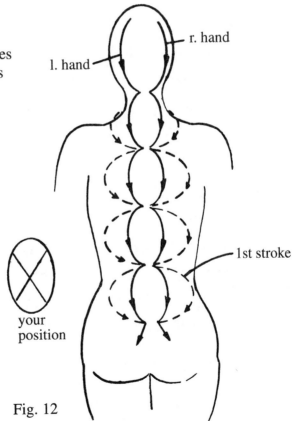

r. hand

l. hand

1st stroke

your position

Fig. 12

Kidneys

The right kidney is positive magnetic in nature. Therefore, you have to place your left hand over the right kidney. The left kidney has a negative charge so your right hand has to be placed on the left kidney.

Have your friend lay on his stomach. Stand to the side of his head and let your hands rest on his kidney. (Fig. 13.)

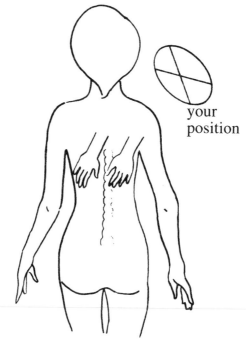

your
position

Fig. 13

Leave hands resting for 2 to 3 minutes, then slowly rotate your hands in the open loop manner towards the spine. The touch must be very light and do it only for 1 minute.

Finally, give the nerves on the spine a little twisting motion. For this you touch a little firmer and in a round, circular motion. Let them know that they have to start working again. After repairing your wiring in the house you turn on the switch. It is the same thing here.

This method is used for older folks when they start to bend forward. In fact, it can be used for anyone with poor posture. It is as if something is pulling them forward from inside. Electrically speaking,

74

the wires are mixed up and constant short cut of electricity makes them pull their bodies forward. Try it and you will be happily surprised.

Stomach

The middle finger of your left hand rests on the "cup," the bones in front of the throat. Place right hand over stomach. Do not place it flat but form a cup out of your hand. (Fig. 14.) Keep this hollow hand for 60 seconds, then make small, soft semicircles over the stomach. Very good in underweight children and adults.

Once daily for 7 days, then 2 times weekly.

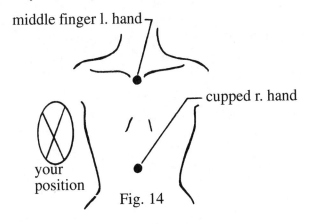

middle finger l. hand

cupped r. hand

your position

Fig. 14

Second Method:

Have your friend sit on a chair. Stand at his left side. Place left hand over stomach so that your fingers touch the gallbladder area. Place right hand on your friend's back so hands are opposite to each other. That means your right hand is more to his right side than just in the middle. (Fig. 15.)

Decongest Your Lungs and Heart

Have your friend lay on his back. You stand at the feet. (Fig. 16.) Softly and slowly stroke both legs from knees down. Shake hands to break the magnetic link, come back in a semicircle to the knees. Do this work for 5 minutes. Strokes must be feather weight, hardly touching the body, and in a slow, rhythmic motion.

The result in congested conditions of heart and lungs is fabulous.

Sleeplessness

Work in the same manner as above, however, over the toes rest for a second. Then shake your hands and start from knees down. Do it in slow, rhythmic, soothing strokes.

Nervousness

When your friend is very nervous, do not give foot compression massage more than once a week. Magneto therapy over the whole body, particularly the soothing spiral, will achieve more satisfying results.

Spleen

The spleen is a very important organ. No wonder God planted it so deeply into our bodies so nothing can happen to this delicate organ. It is the only organ in the body which has two auras. It also is the only organ to be in complete yin-yang balance.

I have studied every available book on this subject, the spleen. A blocked up, congested spleen is a mystery. It is a gland of inner secretion and once the ducts become congested, we are in severe trouble.

An enlarged spleen (greatly the result of congestion) is capable of raising the left rib cage visibly. There is very little pain connected

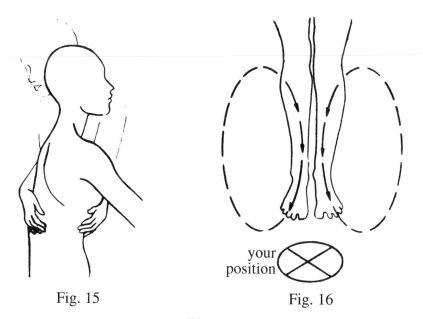

your position

Fig. 15   Fig. 16

with it but fullness and pressure. A sluggish, congested spleen can add to mental instability, depression and stupor. A congested spleen makes a yellow complexion and brown discoloration appears over eyes, cheeks and around mouth. It may effect the heartbeat and often people sigh a lot.

Weakness, disorientation and being afraid of people, cellars, darkness and closed rooms point to troubles in the spleen. People with spleen trouble seem to be more effected by haunted houses and foreign energy possessions and many are obsessed or possessed for years until a helping minister or a psychic steps in to release these poor people of their entities.

To open the congested areas of the spleen, the following method is extremely helpful: Stand at the head of your worktable or slightly at the left side of your friend. Place the fingertips of your right hand under the right armpit. Rest your left hand over his/her solar plexus. (Fig. 17.) Hold your hands in this position until you feel heat or throbbing. Your left hand will feel it more distinctly. Watch the color coming into your friend's face. See the lines in the face smoothing out. Watch the dark discoloration go!

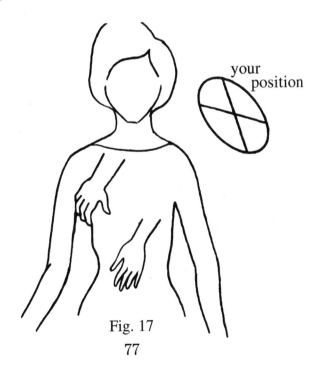

your position

Fig. 17

Do this work after you have made the parallel and the spiral strokes (Fig. 3 and Fig. 4) and do it 7 days in a row. On the second day the patron may expel a sour, putrid stool, black or dark green in color.

Try this simple method on all mentally confused, epileptics or mentally exhausted and on your friends with blood impurities, acne, wrinkles or discolorations of skin in face and arms.

The spleen is the reservoir to store electricity in the body. If the spleen is not in order, the brain takes over this job. However, it has one drawback. People become egocentric. They accomplish nothing worthwhile.

Lymphatic System

The lymphatic system is greatly helped by Swedish massage. Here is an addition to this work of massage therapy and you will like it! You do not have to undress your patron. Just loosen his collar.

Sit on the right side of your friend. Place the fingers of your left hand on the cervicals of his neck. The right hand goes under the left armpit of your friend. (Fig. 18.)

Now relax and feel, imagine and direct with your prayers and your mind the proper flow of the lymphatic system. First, the left hand

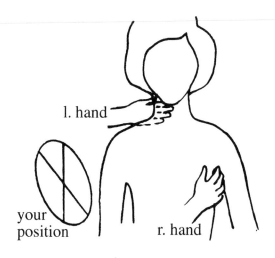

Fig. 18

78

of your friend will become warm and cozy. Secondly, the left foot will be warmer than the right foot and will become cozier. And then the right arm will tingle or become warm. After this you can interrupt your effort. With strokes, brush down the body, front 1 minute and back 1 minute. This work takes 10 to 15 minutes of your time but the result is remarkable.

Wounds will heal faster. Ulcers on the legs will start to heal. Swollen glands start to disappear as the tissue becomes better nourished and the accumulated waste is better expelled.

The lymphatic fluid is very much under the influence of the magnetic field. Every woman adds 3 to 5 pounds of fluid when the moon is full and will lose it 1 or 2 days later. Every hyperactive person becomes super hyper when the moon is at its peak of shining. Sleeping pills are used twice as much and hyperactive children become little devils during this time. We just have not paid too much attention to the electromagnetic influence of the environment and our lymphatic fluid. The laying on of hands in the discussed manner will ease many woes in a simple, remarkable way.

Blood

Your life is in the blood. How often have you heard this and now it comes into the light of electromagnetic knowledge?

The secret power behind the movement of the blood is a great deal of magnetic nature—the movement of each individual blood cell, the disintegration of them, the joining together, the separating, the giving up of energy to each other, the lumping together as in blood clots. Behind all this is electromagnetic power, the secret of the universe, the untapped energies beyond, working in our bloodstream.

The hands directed by the will are the only instruments to direct and correct a faulty magnetic life pattern in the blood. This is the way to influence the faulty electromagnetic pattern when it decides to clot the blood.

Blood Clots:

Have your friend comfortable on the bed or worktable. Flex his knees. Have his hands folded as in prayer but his forefingers should form a pyramid. His thumbs close it. Cover your friend with a light blanket for warmth and comfort. There is nothing like a blanket pulled over you that gives you more security. Now sit on his left side. Spread your arms out so the right hand is over his head. The left hand is slipped under the cover. Hold it close to the tailbone. You cuddle your friend visibly and invisibly. Your hands do not touch the body at all but are 1 inch away from it.

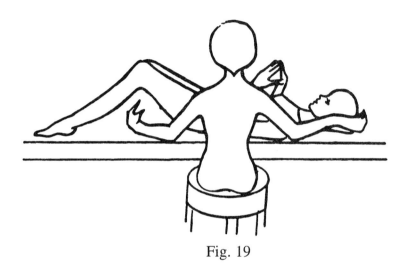

Fig. 19

Now relax and tell your friend to do likewise. With all your heart concentrate on your work. Pray and your energies will be poured into your friend's body. In case someone wants to help you, let him do so by touching your shoulders while standing behind you and also pouring energies through you into the patron's body.

Under your hands the miracle takes place. The blood becomes magnetically charged and the blood clot disintegrates. Visibly, the redness disappears. Also the breathing becomes easier and the fever disappears. (The credit for this method goes to Rev. Dr. F. M. Houston.)

The following story will illustrate. I was invited to a party. I enjoy parties most when I can sit aside and observe the happiness of others. So I did.

A huge man turned to me and out of the blue sky told me that he was a physicist and said, "Please tell me what I can do for myself.

I do not feel well." We sat down and in a flash of a second the Lord showed me that this man had a blood clot just in front of his heart, ready to loosen any minute. I did not know what to say or how to say it when help came by his saying "I did not want to come to this party but an inner voice told me to come." Now I knew this man was a "sensitive" and fully told him what the Lord had revealed to me. "I will look for myself," he said. Then he closed his eyes. When he opened them he stared at me saying, "There is a clot in front of my heart. What can I do?"

Now it was my turn to ask questions and I found out that this man was America's most outstanding scientist and, in addition, a top psychic researcher. Oftentimes he was called to psychic conferences overseas, including Russia.

We found a quiet room and I performed the described magnetic healing on him. Wonder over wonder, this beautiful soul could describe every detail that was going on. He said, "The light from the right hand is blue and white. It goes through the blood. It changes the blood cells with this light. It separates the lumped together blood cells. Now it comes closer to the problem area. It chisels away the problem. First the outsides become light. The blood clot starts to disappear. It disappears like a mist when the sun is coming through." In this moment the scientist took a deep breath and his huge extended chest fell back to normal.

I am the luckiest person on earth to have had such an opportunity to meet a man who could see, actually see and not guess, what was taking place. Thank God for this.

To Stop Bleeding:

To stop bleeding you sit at the right side of your patron. Cradle him by holding the left hand over the head, the right one under the tailbone.

A young physician was drafted to the Vietnam War. When he said goodbye I had the hunch to tell him how to stop bleeding electromagnetically. Two years passed before he returned, a quiet, serene, changed person. "Your advice on how to stop bleeding has saved many soldiers," he stated. "We hardly lost anyone, even in severe injuries and severed arms and legs. It helped." So without great danger and losses the soldiers could be sent back to hospitals in excellent shape.

81

Infection

Break the impact of viral infections by holding deep and steady.

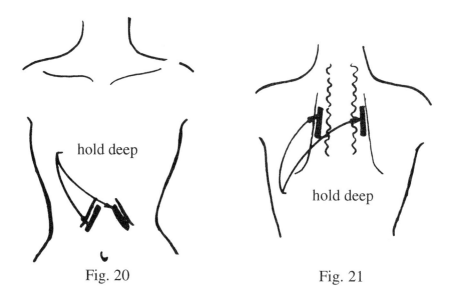

Fig. 20   Fig. 21

Break polio infection next to the shoulder blades. Oftentimes I use a light karate stroke on these congestions near the shoulder blades.

Use Dr. Houston's method for strep infections described in his most wonderful and helpful book, *The Healing Benefits of Acupressure.* It is available at Hanna's Herb Shop, 5684 Valmont Road, Boulder, Colorado 80301.

The Common Cold

The common cold responds favorably to magneto therapy. Have your friend stand or sit. Your right hand lightly touches between his shoulder blades. After 60 seconds rub his back with the spiral movement as mentioned previously. The spirals must be large and cover the width of his back. Do it with the right hand. Have the left one resting on the throat or forehead. (Fig. 22.)

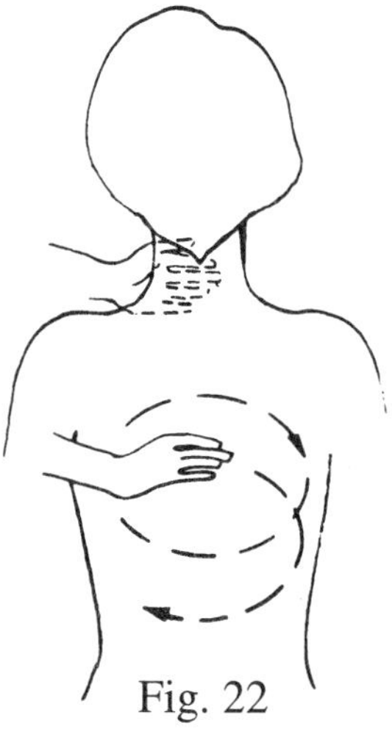

Fig. 22

Pneumonia

When the cold has already settled in the lungs and pneumonia is imminent or already there, the following method of the laying on of hands has saved many, many people.

Place your cupped right hand on the forehead so that the little finger still touches the bridge of the nose. Your left hand rests and cradles the back of the head. Sit comfortably because it will take 10 to 15 minutes. You will hear the congestion break up in the lungs. After that place the right hand on your friend's chest, the left on his back and finish this work with another 5 minutes of your hands.

For all head congestions, headaches and nervous disorders you place the opposite hand (left) on the forehead and the right hand on the back of the head and rest it there another 3 minutes. (Fig. 23.)

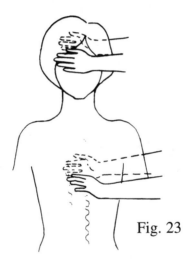

Fig. 23

Sunburn and Other Burns

For several minutes perform light parallel strokes but do not touch the skin. Also, when the skin was subject to cold and partially frozen, it brings life back into it.

Bruises and Other Injuries

Sometimes after someone has broken his leg or arm, has been bandaged and the bandage taken off, the pain still exists. There are two methods to help. The first method: Use strokes lengthwise over injured area not touching anything. The second method (American Indian): Lay middle finger of your right hand beneath the skull of your friend. With the left hand touch the injured limb or other injured part lightly. It is a fantastic method and was and still is used among the tribes of the American Indians.

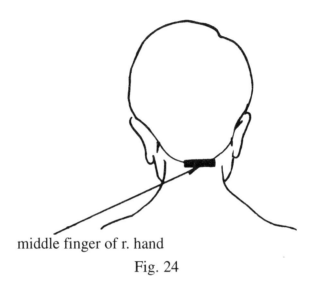

middle finger of r. hand

Fig. 24

All bruises and other injuries respond most favorably to both methods.

Exhaustion

Place a piece of cotton cloth or handkerchief over the person (who is fully clothed). Bring your lips close and firmly right under the heart (tip of heart) and bring "life-breath" into the exhausted person for over 1 minute. Life-breath is done by taking a deep breath and, with the mouth shaped in an "o," quickly expelling the breath in a puff of breath directed at the desired location. Eighteen breaths are needed. The entire blood will be magnetized with life-breath.

For an overly excited person give him life-breath over the stomach where the sternum ends. Soon the excitement will be gone.

The life-breath method is also indicated in fainting spells, convulsions and electroshock therapies. Give aid by lowering the head

84

when pale or lifting the head when red. Then make 20 quick, length-wise strokes. After that give life-breath to heart and stomach both.

Lack of Ability to Concentrate and Emotional Instability

Remember that the lack of concentration in children can be the neglect to cut their fingernails. Too long fingernails have the tendency to hinder the electromagnetic forces. They easily back up and become destructive to the concentration and the development of the inner being of the child.

Women with overly long fingernails have trouble keeping calm and being steady in mood and balance and they are easily upset and lacking in electromagnetic energy in general.

CHAPTER IV

Metals and Other
Poisons
as a
Cause of Ill Health

INTRODUCTION

No machine can be overhauled while the components are in motion. In order that an engine may be repaired, or totally overhauled, all movement of its parts must cease. Unlike the machine, our bodies are endowed with the ability to store sufficient energy to function for considerable time without fuel intake and it is during these periods that nature can heal your body best.

Dissatisfied with methods used in orthodox medicine, with the many, many side effects of drug therapy (which truly is a shock therapy—"shocking the system into balance"), men like Schroth, Kneipp, Kuhne and others came into the limelight. These men and many others like Prof. Brauchle, Dr. Zabel and Dr. Bricher-Benner instructed us to follow the path of nontoxic methods.

However, in their lifetime they did not face catastrophic environmental pollution as atomic fallout, lead poisoning (gasoline), arsenic poisoning (spray) or sodium fluoride poisoning (drinking water). In those times our population did not have the breakdown of the immune system due to poisons, EHF waves, ELF waves, microwaves, computers and televisions. These were unknown. We are confronted with a totally different emergency situation and we, the housewives, have to know this. We have to do our utmost, our very best, to keep our families, our communities and our country healthy.

If you realize that no section of our society is free from the drug menace (even our sportsmen come under its influence), you will agree with me that we women have to stand up and protect our offspring.

Our pioneers in natural cures, as Rev. Kneipp, Prof. Brauchle and many, many others who were dedicated in their service to mankind, only excelled by the mothers of this country who search and search for an answer for their hyperactive children, for an answer for Candida albicans (a disease brought as a side effect of antibiotics and other causes). They search for answers to help their depressed young people, the suicidal tendencies in teen-agers, the fatigue and lethargy in everyone.

The women of this nation, more than ever before, are willing to learn to search and find these answers and their determination will be well rewarded.

Dr. Parcels said, "I found that chemicals and metals cause most of our health problems." She also stated that chemicals destroy the lymphatic system.

We live in a poisoned, chemical treacherous world. We cannot change this but we can help ourselves so that environmental poisons as lead, arsenic, chemicals and pollution do not harm us.

We have to know:

1) Where are the poisons?
2) What harm do they do?
3) How do we recognize them?
4) How do we eliminate them?

ALUMINUM POISONING

Concerned health practitioners in the USA and Canada are urging their patrons to avoid aluminum containing products. Why?

Aluminum has a predisposition to affect neuronal tissue. Many tests done on animals showed that behavior and memory suffered as aluminum levels were increased in lymph and brain.

Many researchers feel that aluminum is the major culprit in Alzheimer's disease, a disease of dementia, forgetfulness and senility. Autopsies showed that individuals afflicted with Alzheimer's disease had accumulated 6 times as much aluminum in the brain as healthy people.

I urge you to not take a chance. Throw away your aluminum pots and your beer and soft drinks in aluminum containers. Dr. Berlyne, Ben Ari and others stated, "The practice of cooking in aluminum utensils and wrapping foods in aluminum foil may result in gross changes in the aluminum content of food before ingestion." Aluminum is also found in:

- Antacids
- Baking powder
- Toothpaste
- Antiperspirants

Also, numerous cities add aluminum salt to drinking water to reduce the cloudiness of it. It makes the water cosmetically pleasing.

Symptoms of aluminum poisoning may include:

- Dryness of mouth
- Stomach pain
- Stomach ulcers
- Hard stool and/or small hardened pieces or "feces stones"
- Pain in spleen area
- Forgetfulness
- Children cry a lot
- Kidney problem, especially the right kidney

What to Do:

Antidote No. I:
Homeopathic *Alumina 6x to 12x*

Antidote No. II:
Herbal formula:
- Pumpkin Seed
- Okra
- Rhubarb root
- Capsicum
- Peppermint
- Dulse

Antidote No. III:
A product from Coenzyme International

These are coenzyme minerals in an aqueous extraction of naturally chelated colloidal minerals. These minerals are derived from an ancient seabed mineral deposit. The action of colloidal aluminum with other enzymes removes aluminum deposits on the order of God's law that "like attracts like."

Many illnesses, including tumors good or bad, are in the end aluminum accumulations. By removing and transmuting aluminum, the body can rid itself from all kinds of troubles. This is the teaching of Dr. John Ray.

ARSENIC POISONING

Many household and garden pesticides contain arsenoxide.

Acute arsenic poisoning has to be treated at once in the emergency room and is not the place to be mentioned here. However, chronic arsenic poisoning is rarely discovered and hardly ever discussed.

Here are the chronic arsenic poisoning symptoms:

- Sweetish metallic taste
- Garlicky odor to breath and stool
- Constriction of throat
- Difficulties in swallowing
- Burning pains in esophagus, stomach and sometimes bowels
- Muscle spasms
- Pain in muscles of back
- Spine is pulled out of line so that people have to go for adjustments over and over again (adjustments do not hold); Elkium and Faky said arsenic, the element arsenic, is an active enzyme inhibiter
- Mild gastrointestinal disturbances
- Anorexia
- Low grade fever (changes in white blood count)
- Weakness
- Catarrhal symptoms (nose, throat, eyes)
- Brittle nails
- Loss of hair
- Localized edema in the eyelids signifies problems in the liver, possibly due to arsenic
- Nervousness

Since arsenic has a constricting effect on the muscle structure and loves to lodge in muscles, the most outstanding symptom is the constant backache.

Arsenic also settles in the brain, dislodging the phosphorus which is needed for proper brain functioning.

What to Do:

If you can find Mexican raw sugar, take 1 tsp. 3 times daily. Homeopathic *Arsenicum metallicum 6x* does the job. The herbal combination of pumpkin seed, okra, rhubarb root, capsicum, peppermint and dulse transmutes almost all metals.

Very helpful is the herb from Southern and Eastern Africa called *Harpagophytum procumbens* (devil's claw). This tea washes out metallic poisons as well as chemical poisons. It carries the rare combination of three active ingredients: Flukoside, fruran, and pyror.

There is an old-time natural remedy used over centuries and centuries that can be found in the book *Biochemical Toxicology* by Ernest Hodgson and Frank Guthrie.

CADMIUM POISONING

Although cadmium is found in foods, the levels are too low to be of any toxicological significance. Cadmium has many industrial uses, for example, electroplating, low melting alloys, low friction, fatigue resistant bearing alloys, solders, batteries, pigments and as a barrier in atomic fission control. Therefore, it is to be expected that low to moderate cadmium content of the environment is widespread. Since chronic exposure to even low levels of trace elements can lead to health problems, cadmium is of particular concern to those concerned with environmental quality.

Industrial exposure is the most prevalent cause of chronic and acute cadmium toxicity. Chronic toxicity is manifested in humans by anosmia as a result of olfactory nerve damage, kidney dysfunction and emphysema. Cadmium has also been implicated as a possible cause of lung cancer. The cadmium content of tobacco leaves is significant but there is no experimental evidence linking cadmium in tobacco to emphysema and lung cancer. It has been suggested that cadmium may play a role in the production of arteriosclerosis, hypertension and cardiovascular disease but the data are limited and contradictory. It is worth noting that the body's burden of cadmium in smokers is 1½ to 2 times than that of nonsmokers.

Acute cadmium toxicity in humans often leads to pneumonitis ranging from severe to fatal. Vomiting, diarrhea and prostration are also symptoms of acute cadmium poisoning.

Cadmium affects the activities of several enzymes. Enhanced activity of 6-amino levulinic acid dehydratase, pyruvate dehydrogenase and pyruvate decarboxylase have been noted, while depressed activity of 6-amino levulinic acid synthetase, alcohol dehydrogenase, aryl sulfatase and lipoamide dehydrogenase result from cadmium intoxication.

Cadmium has been shown to interact with phospholipids, such as phosphatidylserine and phosphatidylethanolamine. These interactions may be responsible for the toxic effects of cadmium on membranes.

Cadmium settles predominantly in heart and right kidney.

Answer:
- More zinc intake
- More paprika
- And, best of all, homeopathic *Cadmium metallicum* in low potency *(6x to 30x)*

References:
Nordberg, G. F. (Ed.). Effects and Dose-Response Relationships of Toxic Metals. Amsterdam: Elsevier, 1976.
Symposium on biological and pharmacological effects of metal contaminants. Fed. Proc. 27(1977), 15.

LEAD POISONING

Lead is still one of the more commonly used toxic heavy metals but its modern use is not nearly so diverse as during the 17th through the 19th centuries. The gastrointestinal absorption of lead varies with age; adults absorb 5 to 10 percent of an oral dose, whereas children may absorb up to 50 percent of an oral dose. Lead is stored in the liver and bone, particularly bone, where it accumulates over a period of many years, if not throughout the lifetime.

Exposure to lead takes on many forms in addition to that of industrial hazards. Although lead intake from paints, water pipes, tin cans and insecticides has decreased, exposure to other forms of lead, such as in motor vehicle exhausts and tobacco smoke, has either stabilized or increased. Intake of lead paint by children is still a problem in poor urban neighborhoods where lead containing painted surfaces still remain. Lead poisoning has been reported in the Southern USA as a result of the consumption of non-taxed, distilled alcoholic beverages, commonly known as moonshine.

Symptoms of lead poisoning include abdominal pain, anemia and lesions of the central and peripheral nervous systems. The lesions of the central nervous system cause behavioral problems. The anemia is characterized by a larger than normal number of erythrocytes and is of the hypochromic, microcytic type.

The principal biochemical effect of lead intoxication in humans and animals is defective hemoglobin synthesis. Lead inhibits iron incorporation into protoporphyrin which results in lower heme concentrations and higher protoporphyrin concentrations in erythrocytes. Excretion of coproporphyrin is increased and the iron content of the blood plasma and bone marrow is elevated. Lead also interferes with an earlier step in heme synthesis by inhibiting 6-amino levulinic acid dehydratase which converts 6-amino levulinic acid to prophobilinogen. The resulting increase of 6-amino levulinic acid in blood and urine is a sensitive indicator of plumbism. In advanced lead poisoning, synthesis of the globin moiety of hemoglobin is also inhibited.

Lead is a protoplasmic poison. That means it interferes with the proper life-energy-enzyme exchange in the living body. It is amazing how beautifully our system is able to take this load of lead poisoning. Everyone has it. Only a few people in very isolated places in the mountains or prairies are free from lead intoxication.

There is to be considered: 1) The amount of lead in our system; 2) the tolerance factor of lead, arsenic, cadmium, mercury, copper and other heavy metals. This tolerance factor differs in everyone. Some people sponge in more arsenic than others, some more lead, some more aluminum-lead and some more mercury. I found redheaded people are prone to take in more copper than others. And orientals take in more mercury. The fair people take in more lead and aluminum. The individual tolerance also differs widely. In every case of leukemia the tolerance level of arsenic should be checked. In every case of exhaustion the lead level should be checked.

It is said that the fall of Rome was nothing more than the accumulated lead poisoning in all of its citizens. They used to carry their water in lead pipes and lead containers and the accumulated lead destroyed the nation. Our water pipes are safe but how about the air we breathe? Are the cities and the crowded highways safe?

On windless days you can see the car exhausts lingering over our highways. In a long stripe of grey-blue it lies here like a monster. In fact, it is a monster which eats up our health. When lead is taken in through the lungs, it is more likely to be in suspension in the fluids of the body, like the lymphatic fluid, the blood and the gland fluids. When eaten with food as the Romans did, it is more likely to be deposited in joints, liver, pancreas and heart.

The Biologisch-Physicalische Research Institute in Obergensingen, West Germany reports that the lead contamination of the atmosphere is increasingly alarming. Every third patient shows lead poisoning. Most probably the car exhaust is at fault in this misery. Every gallon of gasoline contains 60 mg of lead. Approximately 8,000 tons of this metal lead is puffed into the atmosphere every year. In the streets children and small animals are particularly exposed to the dangers of poisons through heavy metal accumulations in the atmosphere, since these metals have a tendency to settle down.

The scientists of Obergensingen developed an instrument which enables them to test 1,000 blood samples a day. Desperately, they try to find the antidote to the accumulations of lead residue in humans and animals. Their findings are widely publicized to change the condition of air pollution at least in their country.

The lead tragedy in our country and all civilized countries started in 1922 when Mighty and Boyd added lead ethyl to the gasoline.

The balance quota of lead in America is 0.002 mg/m^3 which can be as high as 60 times in rush hour traffic. See Dr. Stafin's *Stomach and Intestine Research.* Out of 5 to 10 percent of dust which the lung takes in, 50 percent of it is lead dust which is particularly detrimental to children. Lead is stored in children in the coverings of the bones and joints. It has an affinity to the lipoids and stores in the nervous system and in the brain.

Lead poisoning can interfere with enzyme processes by displacing the essential mineral nucleus or by precipitating the enzymes together (gluing them).

Because of the changes in the biochemistry of the body due to heavy metal toxins, it is extremely important to take an extra supply of essential minerals.

The most serious manifestation is lead encephalopathy which requires prompt and skillful treatment. Increased intracranial pressure may occur suddenly and must be treated vigorously.

Encephalopathy is very serious. It causes a mortality rate of 25 percent or more and often leaves mental retardation and various permanent neurologic lesions in those who survive. In adults, permanent blindness, extraocular muscle paralysis or other lesions may result. The acute form caused by tetraethyl lead either is fatal or is followed by complete recovery. There is great urgency in treatment of this form. One cannot wait to get results of lead analysis before starting treatment.

What to Do:

When lead is attaching and being stored in the nervous system, the following symptoms are observed:

- Mad, weakened constitution
- Lack of will power
- Lack of abstract thinking
- More tooth decay
- Allergic reactions to food and environment

Lead is stored in kidneys, liver, bone marrow and spleen which causes an increase in diabetes, multiple sclerosis, tooth decay or lack of mental capacity.

What can we do to detoxify our bodies from lead?

You are the only one who can do something about it. Here are some recipes for you:

1)   2 qt cranberry juice
         3 tsp. whole cloves
         2 tsp. ground cinnamon
         1 tsp. cream of tartar

Boil the cloves in 1 qt cranberry juice for 20 minutes. Strain and add 2 tsp. ground cinnamon. Stir and add it to the rest of the cranberry juice. Now add 1 tsp. cream of tartar. Stir. Drink 8 oz 3 times daily for 12 to 15 days. For children, 6 oz 2 times daily for 12 to 15 days. Then, do it once a week.

2)   A wonderful herbal formula for taking out lead residue is:
         6 oz basil
         1 oz rosemary
         1 oz hyssop
         1 oz boneset

3)   As mentioned previously, the herbal combination of:

Pumpkin seed
Okra
Rhubarb root
Capsicum
Peppermint
Dulse

4)   A combination of cloves and vitamin C will combat the problem of lead in the body. Researchers and doctors have made numerous statements about the terrible effects of lead in the tissues and that it is everywhere and almost all persons have some lead in them. It has been found that cloves and vitamin C do an excellent job of neutralizing this prevalent situation. Also, some colds and flu respond to this combination.

Scientific Studies of Lead and Mercury
Levels in Emotionally Disturbed Children

Children exposed to toxic amounts of lead and other metal pollutants are subject to severe behavioral disorders resulting from damage to the central nervous system (Byers and Lord, 1943; Pfeiffer, 1977). It remains to be determined whether sub-toxic metal levels are an etiologic agent in behavioral disorders. Sub-toxic lead levels previously thought harmless are now being associated with hyperactivity, impulsiveness, short attention span and immaturity.

In Wyoming an outstanding examination of schoolchildren with learning and behavioral problems was performed and I am bringing this knowledge to you. . . . After obtaining parental permission, children were asked to submit a small sample of hair (about 400 mg) for trace minerals analysis. Hair samples were collected from the nape of each child's neck, as close to the scalp as possible, by the senior researcher using stainless steel scissors. The hair samples were submitted to a state licensed clinical laboratory where they were analyzed with three instruments—the atomic absorption spectrophotometer, the graphite furnace and the induction-coupled plasma torch—to determine five toxic metal levels. The five toxic metal levels tested for were lead, mercury, arsenic, cadmium and aluminum.

Precise laboratory techniques were used to assure reliability requirements. The two groups of children showed the following results:

Metal	Emotionally disturbed children:	Control Group
Lead	10.78 parts per million	2.76 ppm
Mercury	1.30 ppm	.47 ppm
Arsenic	2.74 ppm	1.35 ppm
Cadmium	.75 ppm	.37 ppm
Aluminum	12.62 ppm	.00 ppm

The data of this study does not establish a causative relationship but shows an association between lead and mercury concentrations and behavioral deficiency in children.

Recent neurochemical studies of Dr. Silbergeld and Houshka (1980) showed that lead and mercury are potent neurotoxins. Their effects are demonstrated in the neuronal system by using tests with acetylcholine, catecholamines and GABA (gamma-aminobutyric acid) as transmitters.

Looking back to the toxic metal chart, you will notice that the aluminum level of disturbed children is very high, while nonexistent in the control group. In my personal opinion, this has to be noted and needs further studies by leading scientists which were *not* done in this test evaluation.

The studies of these scientists are very important and they caution us not to assume that there is a "safe" level of lead and mercury exposure because there is concern that neurons may be irreversibly damaged by an exposure to lead and also mercury.

General

Edmund B. Fink summarizes that many features of poisoning by heavy metals are similar but the important metals from the standpoint of toxicology are arsenic, lead, mercury and others. You may find his collection of knowledge in his book *Diseases Due to Chemical Factors.*

Lead May Have Hastened the Fall of Rome

BOSTON (AP)—Two-thirds of the emperors of ancient Rome may have been poisoned and even mentally unhinged by high doses of lead in their wine and food, and that could have hastened the fall of the Roman Empire, a study concludes.

A researcher calculated that Roman aristocrats consumed six times as much lead as modern safety standards allow, and he said many of them had gout, a disease that can be caused by lead poisoning.

The idea that lead poisoning caused Rome to fall has been proposed before, but Nriagu has put together a large amount of evidence that is being published as a book. A summary of his findings was printed in the *New England Journal of Medicine*.

Lead can cause mental retardation and a variety of personality changes.

Dr. Jane S. Lin-Fu, a lead expert at the Health Services Administration of the Department of Health and Human Services in Rockville, Md., agrees. "From a public health standpoint, we have to set levels to protect the most vulnerable," she said.

"Many children found to have undue lead absorption receive no treatment and Dr. Needleman's study showed that subtle psychological damage occurs in some children at very low lead levels," Dr. Lin-Fu noted. "Will they become the school failures and drop-outs of tomorrow, the juvenile delinquents of the future?"

Dr. Lin-Fu added that "adults may also sustain fairly subtle changes, such as increased irritability or decreased ability to concentrate, when exposed to low lead levels."

Dr. Silbergeld pointed out that the brain is relatively well protected from lead, although less so in the developing fetus and young children than in adults. Nonetheless, she added, once lead gets into a brain cell, it binds tightly to critical cell parts and can't be removed. Rather than killing the cell outright, the cell continues to function but abnormally, she explained.

Furthermore, even when lead does not affect the brain directly, Dr. Silbergeld's studies with Dr. Julian Chisholm at Johns Hopkins University have shown that derangements in blood formation indirectly disrupt a substance called GABA, a major transmitter of nerve messages in the brain. This disruption can occur at very low levels of lead, she said. Children in some cities have amounts of lead in their blood that represent "undue lead absorption" as defined by the Public Health Service. This level results in biochemical abnormalities, but no clear symptoms of lead poisoning.

In addition, about 20 percent of youngsters are exposed to lead in the low-level amounts recently shown to produce decrements in intelligence and behavioral abnormalities, including hyperactivity in some children, according to a widely regarded study headed by Dr. Herbert L. Needleman at Children's Hospital Medical Center in Boston.

Studies by Dr. Patterson and Dorothy Settle at the California Institute of Technology have shown that all official estimates of the amounts of lead in the natural environment are hundreds or thousands of times too high because the measurement techniques used by federal agencies contaminate the sample with lead. This has resulted in an extreme underestimation of the amount of lead introduced by human activities, the researchers said.

MERCURY POISONING

"Mercury occurs as a bright, shining, silver white metal, liquid at ordinary temperatures, and easily divisible into globules. Mercury has a specific gravity of about 13.5. Mercury is insoluble in the ordinary solvents, in hydrochloric acid, and at ordinary temperatures in sulfuric acid, but it is soluble in the latter upon boiling. It is readily and completely soluble in nitric acid." N.F.XI.

Since mercury ion precipitates protein, mercuric salts are protoplasmic poisons and metallic mercury and its various compounds are at least potentially so. The toxicity, and often the action, of mercury compounds is proportional to the content of mercuric ion. Mercury and its salts and other compounds have been variously used, as antiseptics, parasiticides, fungicides, antiluetic agents, diuretics and catharsis.

Absorption and Elimination

Metallic mercury in bulk is not absorbed but when it is dispersed in very small globules having a large total surface area or when it is present in the form of a salt or certain other of its compounds, it is absorbed by the mucosa of the alimentary tract. It is also absorbed through the skin and by inhalation as vapor. Mercury is excreted chiefly through the kidneys and the colon, although it has been detected in practically every secretion of the body; thus, it is found in sweat, bile and milk. Elimination is comparatively slow. While most of a dose of mercury is excreted during the first week, the excretion nevertheless continues for months. Intake of as little as 0.4 mg of mercury daily may result in poisoning.

The equivalent of 500 mg of mercury was found in the liver and kidneys of a man who had not received treatment for several months prior to his death. It was also found in the spleen, intestinal walls, heart, skeletal muscles, lungs and bones. When present in blood in higher concentrations, it acts as a local irritant and leads to increased glandular secretion. The salivary glands are the most sensitive, so that ptyalism is an early symptom of chronic mercury poisoning, however, the kidneys and bowels are affected also.

Mercury was the first antisyphilitic drug which had real therapeutic action. It is not used any longer for that purpose.

At one time mercurials were highly regarded for their antiphlogistic (anti-inflammatory) action in the treatment of inflammations of membranes as in pleurisy, iritis and peritonitis, especially when the exudate was of a fibrinous nature.

Edmund Fink writes, "Mercury ions even in fairly diluted solutions denature protein and cause protein precipitation. Mercury poisoning can make damage to the basal ganglia of the brain which can induce Parkinson-like symptoms."

The term "erethism" is applied to the psychic disturbance characterized by irritability, shyness and deterioration of family and social activities, suggesting mercury or other metal poisoning.

Since makers of felt hats formerly used mercury salts in the manufacturing process and often became "mad," these symptoms gave rise to the phrase "mad as a hatter."

Symptoms of chronic mercury poisoning include:

• Excessive salivation and a metallic taste.
• A blue line develops along the gingival margin.
• Gums become hypertrophied, bleed easily and are sore.
• Teeth become loose.
• Tremors of the eyelids, lips, tongue, fingers and extremities are characteristic of chronic poisoning.
• Coarse, jerky movements and gross incoordination interfere with fine movements such as writing and eating.

• Atrophy of the cerebellar cortex and, to a lesser extent, of the cerebral cortex occurs.

• Microscopic changes occur in the granular layer of the cerebellum, ganglion cells and posterior columns.

Mercurial Intoxication

Ethyl and methyl compounds of mercury are used for fungal diseases of cereals and grain. These compounds have an affinity for the central nervous system and produce:

• Generalized ataxia
• Tremors
• Deafness
• Loss of coordination
• Eczema, allergy
• Anxiety, mental depression
• Progressive visual deterioration
• Loss of memory
• Insomnia
• Loss of hearing
• Suicidal tendency
• Coma and death

Changes in the central nervous system similar to the lesions of chronic mercury poisoning are found.

Hypersensitivity

Hypersensitivity reactions to mercurial diuretic agents include asthma, urticaria, exfoliative dermatitis and sudden death.

Kidney Troubles

Contact with ammoniated mercury and other compounds has caused proteinuria and nephrotic syndrome.

ENVIRONMENTAL METALLIC POISONING (SUCH AS LEAD, ARSENIC, ALUMINUM, MERCURY, ETC.)

The 3-Day Diet

This diet relieves the body of environmental poisons. Take:

Green beans	3 lb
Zucchini	4 lb
Parsley	3 bunches
Celery	2 lb

Boil the green beans in plenty of water until done. Add finely chopped celery and coarsely cut zucchini. Boil another 5 minutes or until the zucchini is done. Take from the fire and add 3 bunches of finely chopped parsley. Season with spice or another herb flavor. This is all you eat, and all you will want, for the next 3 days. Eat this until it is all gone. Make more if needed. When reheating, take only a portion from the refrigerator and eat all you want. Eat the mixture as often as you want. Drink parsley tea or willow leaf tea as a beverage.

Use this diet when metals are lodged in your glands and nerves. More iron food. More calcium food.

Antidotes to ...

Metallic poison lead	Green beans and zucchini	Zucchini and green beans eaten exclusively for 3 days. This will get rid of metallic poisons.
Metallic poisons aluminum and arsenic	Squash Strawberries	Removes arsenic poisons. Extra good for smokers. It also removes other metallic poisons.
Metallic poison arsenic	Mexican raw sugar	Removes Arsenic poisons. Take 1 tsp. several times daily until symptoms subside.

Vitamin C is also needed to counteract environmental poisons. Dr. Linus Pauling (Stanford University) stated that Vitamin C stimulates interferon production. Interferon is needed to strengthen the immune system.

Algae is a terrific help to counteract environmental poisons. Red algae bind plutonium poison.

Brown alga binds strontium 90 and cadmium poisons.

Green alga binds calcium and mercury poisons.

Pectin from citrus binds metals to some extent. Eat the whole fruit.

Pollen, ¼ tsp. 2 times daily, has proven to bind environmental poisons.

Chamomile is very helpful to drink for lead poisoning. Chamomile is soothing to the nerves. It has a lot of calcium in it, so it is very good for young children, especially in getting them to replace the lead with calcium in the body.

Toxic Metal Levels Chart

Toxic Metal	Aluminum
Protective Nutrients	Vitamins E and C, herbal combination of pumpkin seed, okra, rhubarb root, capsicum, peppermint and dulse
Sources in Environment	Aluminum cooking utensils, antacids, foils, deodorants, aluminum sulfate baking powders, processed foods containing aluminum, soft water
Interferes with Bodily Functions	Irritating to gut, affects bone formation and brain, dry mouth, dry stools, cell oxydation inhibition
Toxicity Symptoms	Gastrointestinal irritation, colic, rickets, convulsions

Toxic Metal	Arsenic
Protective Nutrients	Iodine, selenium, sulfur, amino acids, vitamin C
Sources in Environment	Coal burning, pesticides, insecticides, herbicides, defoliants, metal smelting, cigarette smoke, manufacture of glass, mirrors, pesticides, insecticides, herbicides and defoliants
Interferes with Bodily Functions	Metabolic inhibitor (reduces energy production efficiency), cellular and enzyme poison
Toxicity Symptoms	Fatigue, low vitality, listlessness, loss of pain sensation, loss of body hair, skin color changes, dark spots, gastroenteritis, back pain

Toxic Metal	Cadmium
Protective Nutrients	Zinc, calcium, sulfur, amino acids, vitamin C
Sources in Environment	Cigarette smoke, oxide dusts, contaminated drinking water, galvanized pipes, paints, welding, pigments, contaminated shellfish from industrial seashores
Interferes with Bodily Functions	Heart and blood vessel structure (hypertension), kidneys, blocks appetite and smell centers, calcium metabolism, removes calcium from bones
Toxicity Symptoms	Hypertension, kidney damage, loss of sense of smell, decreased appetite

Toxic Metal	Lead
Protective Nutrients	Sulfur, amino acids, vitamins C and E, calcium, iron
Sources in Environment	Leaded gas, lead based paint, newsprint and colored ads, hair dyes and rinses, dolomite, soft coal, leaded glass, pewter ware, pesticides, pencils, fertilizers, pottery, cosmetics, tobacco smoke, polluted air (average 35 mg/day in USA, higher in industrial areas and some cities).
Interferes with Bodily Functions	Enzyme poison, osteoblast production, blood formation, blocks enzymes at cell level
Toxicity Symptoms	Weakness, listlessness, fatigue, pallor, abdominal discomfort, constipation, hyperactive children

Toxic Metal	Mercury
Protective Nutrients	Pectin, sulfur, amino acids, vitamin C, selenium
Sources in Environment	Manufacture and delivery of petroleum products, fungicides, fluorescent lamps, cosmetics, hair dyes, barometers, thermometers, amalgams in dentistry, salt water fish caught in contaminated waters
Interferes with Bodily Functions	Destroys cells, blocks transport of sugars (energy at cell levels), increases permeability of potassium (convulsions)
Toxicity Symptoms	Loss of appetite and weight, severe emotional disturbances, tremors, blood changes, inflammation of gums, chewing and swallowing difficulty, loss of sense of pain

Strontium 90 + Cesium

These came into our lives through nuclear testing. Strontium 90 may be nullified by the intake of biological calcium as calcium orotate, calcium phosphate *(cell salt #2)* and calcium sulfate *(cell salt #3)*. *See* Ch. I (Neglect as a Cause of Ill Health: Cell Salts (Tissue Salts)).

Sulfur Baths

One of the most universal remedies to remove lead, arsenic, platinum, gold and mercury from your body is sulfur baths. The sulfur baths in Europe are overcrowded. Many Americans find help there. Every summer a stream of Americans fly to European spas to take care of their problems with health. We have these wonderful healing waters right here in this country. They are undiscovered and unattended. The precious water runs away into the beautiful wilderness. A national campaign should be started to build beautiful spas around these precious sulfur waters of America. It should be made available to rich and poor alike.

Thanks to the advancement of industry, sulfur baths are available in dry form and the granules or tablets or powders can be added to the bath water once a month, particularly for women.

Cranberry juice is very good to remove toxins from the body. A suggested way is 4 oz cranberry juice and 4 oz distilled water. Take this mixture 4 times daily for 3 days, then wait about 5 days and repeat. About 120 units of toxins can be eliminated daily with this program.

FLUORINE POISONING

Symptoms of Chronic Fluorine Poisoning

The *National Fluoridation News*—Jan. 1955, article by Dr. G. L. Waldbott, Detroit, Michigan, states: "A peculiar disease is making its appearance throughout the land. When those affected seek medical advice, doctors who are not yet familiar with this disease are liable to call them neurotics; they may even ridicule them. It is the initial stage of chronic fluorine poisoning." As a rule patients complain of:

- Irritation of the mouth with sores and ulcers.
- Predisposition to upper respiratory infections.
- Continuous backache along the spinal cord. Spine becomes stiff.
- Sharp, gnawing pains in the stomach, as though it were "burning inside."
- Nausea and loss of appetite.
- The more water you drink, the more discomfort in the stomach.
- Mental alertness deteriorates. Can't think clearly.

- Numbness and weakness in the legs and arms, especially in the fourth and fifth fingers.
- Feel unsteady. Sometimes legs give way. May fall down.
- Skin shows dry eruptions (seborrhea) on chest.

Dr. Leo Spira, who conducted experiments with fluorine on rats for 4 years, found that:

- Fluorine interferes with the proper utilization of vitamin B.
- Much damage was done to the kidneys, causing Bright's disease.
- The thyroid gland was greatly damaged by the action of fluorine.
- Fluorine caused the heart muscles to become flabby and degenerated.

The 1983 United States Pharmacoepia Volumes on Drug Information list the following that can occur among people taking tablets containing ½ to 1 mg of fluoride per day (this is the amount of fluoride found in 1 to 2 pints of fluoridated water):

- Black, tarry stools
- Stiffness
- Bloody vomit
- Diarrhea
- Faintness
- Nausea and vomiting
- Shallow breathing
- Stomach cramps or pain
- Tremors
- Unusual excitement
- Unusual increase in saliva
- Watery eyes
- Weakness
- Constipation
- Loss of appetite
- Pain and aching of bones
- Skin rash
- Sores in the mouth and on the lips

Fluoride Constitution

With permission from Dr. John Yiamouyiannis, I took these drawings from his incredible book, *Fluoride: The Aging Factor,* published by Health Action Press. You will have the revelation of your life. When you read it, you will find many of the answers you have been searching for. *See* Ch. VIII (Collection of Knowledge: Recommended Readings).

• Fluoride disturbs the chromosome repair enzyme so the chromosome looks like this:

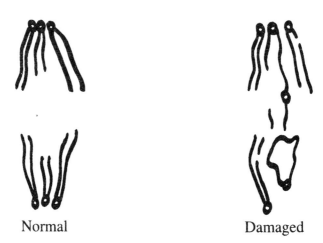

Normal   Damaged

• Sodium fluoride damages the immune system by weakening it as an old body is weakened (old age problem).
• Sodium fluoride interrupts the amino acid chain in collagen.

One of the most terrifying things fluoride does is turn the thought process into slow motion.

Fluoride is used to calm rioting prisoners. Watts Riot in Los Angeles was beaten down when excess fluoride was added to the drinking water. Fluoride does not taste, not even in toothpaste. In one tube of toothpaste so much fluoride is added that one child could die from eating one tube of toothpaste.

If we want to medicate our drinking water, let us do it on an individual basis. It is against the constitution of America to force some stuff down the throat.

Many years ago, when kidney dialysis machines were far-out and seldom used, Denver had one of the first centers.

A physician from Houston, Texas lived with us for a while and he had a treatment every other day. He was so miserable, so sick, so disappointed, so down, that the only thing that was of any help was stroking his tortured body lightly, hardly touching him.

One day I told him that the trouble was fluoride poisoning. He sat up in bed, his eyes widened. "Now I see the connection," he said.

"I wanted to have fluoride in the drinking water in Texas. In order to show and demonstrate the safeness of it, I drank a full glass of rather much fluoride concentrated water. Nothing happened, but. . . . A few days later, I had pain in the kidneys. I never connected it with that brave deed. Please help me to get it out of my kidneys," he asked. I failed. Even so, I prayed for hours for this man. He died.

The following information is taken from the book *Introduction to Biochemical Toxicology* by Ernest Hodgson and Frank Guthrie.

Fluoride inhibits glycolysis but has no effect on oxygen consumption. Pronounced hyperglycemia and glycosuria are induced in rabbits by sodium fluoride. The hyperglycemia is reversible by insulin. Fluoride ion inhibits cholinesterase and several phosphatases and interferes with the metabolization of arginine and glutamine. Fluoroacetate is a metabolic poison by virtue of its strong inhibition of the tricarboxylic acid cycle. Fluoroacetate combines with oxaloacetic acid to form fluorocitric acid which blocks tricarboxylic acid cycle activity and causes citric acid to accumulate in the tissues.

Sodium Fluoride

Sodium fluoride destroys our will to live. It settles in the neck on the left side and in the tissue and causes you not to care. People are mentally lethargic. It promotes low blood sugar.

Since fluoride accumulates in the kidneys, kidneys have to have special attention. In an adult, through osmosis, the fluoride in toothpaste *can* offset the iodine in the thyroid and the calcium hormones in the parathyroid in such a manner that the glandular system suffers. Also, the sugar system becomes unstable.

Dr. John Yiamouyiannis stated that fluoride interrupts the chain of amino acid in collagen.

Researchers from Harvard University and the National Institutes of Health knew in the 1960s that fluoride disrupted collagen synthesis. It was not until 1979 to 1981, however, that a new flurry of research activity in this area began.

109

Collagen is composed of amino acids linked together in a chain. However, collagen contains two additional amino acids, hydroxyproline and hydroxylysine, not found in other proteins. Thus, when collagen synthesis is interfered with or when collagen breaks down, the hydroxyproline and hydroxylysine levels in the blood and urine increase breakdown of the collagen protein chain into its amino acid links. Thus, the high levels of the "free" hydroxyproline and hydroxylysine "links" induced by fluoride is conclusive evidence that fluoride is accelerating the breakdown of collagen.

What to do:

What to do when sodium fluoride has taken hold in you? We have two distinct formulas to help. Dr. S. Waksman, in his lengthy laboratory experiments, found that manganese reduces the toxic effect of sodium fluoride considerably. So much so that manganese is now used widely all over the country.

Another big, big help is a tasty tea made out of:

- Calendula
- Dandelion leaves
- Elder
- Nettle
- Red root
- St. John's wort
- Yarrow

Sodium fluoride reduces the effectiveness of lactobacillus acidophilus which forms cariogenic lactic acid. This acid is needed to manufacture your own interferon, which is most important to fight cancer.

Cottage cheese mixed with raw oils makes your own interferon. *See* Ch. VI (Infections as a Cause of Ill Health: Make Your Own Interferon).

PLUTONIUM

Raw plutonium stones are not harmful. They only become harmful when they are tampered with, isolated or split. Plutonium explodes into 3 parts in 1½ days when it enters the air. Two of the parts are positively charged. They get into our bodies and cut the proteins, enzymes and molecules into little pieces which float in the bloodstream and lymphatic system.

RADIATION

Peat moss removes radiation (x-ray, cancer, radiation cobalt, fallout). A 4- to 6-inch bed of peat moss removes all radiation from the body in one night. Fifty to 100 pound sacks of moss are sold like dirt. It can be put under the bed or in flower pots and is good for ½ year under or around the TV. Willow leaves are another radiation antidote. Miso, which is fermented bean paste, will protect you from radiation. Don't boil it.

In Hiroshima, after the A-bomb, people ate tomatoes and cucumbers for 3 months to clear the fallout from their systems.

PESTICIDES

Most pesticides are stored in the fatty deposits of the human body. By undertaking a fat reducing diet, these pesticides can bring on heart attack and/or severe nervous disorder. Therefore, take it easy with reducing diets.

IRRADIATED FOOD

The controversy grows. This past year, the use of the pesticide EDB on grains and fruits was banned because the chemical was found to cause cancer in animals. Last February, the Food and Drug Administration (FDA) proposed a possible alternative. The agency wants to allow the use of ionizing radiation—such as that emitted by x-ray machines—to kill pests on fruits, vegetables and spices. Now the question being asked is: Will acceptance of the proposal simply substitute one problem for another?

The FDA says no, based on 30 years of governmentally funded studies. It maintains that food irradiation is safe when used at doses not exceeding 100 kilorads. (A rad is a unit used to express an amount of absorbed radiation.) The agency claims that the process leaves no detectable radioactive residue on food and does not significantly reduce nutritional content. In addition, it can extend the shelf life of certain foods, such as potatoes and oranges, by inhibiting sprouting or ripening.

But opponents of food irradiation argue that the safety of the process has not been firmly proved.

Radiation causes chemical changes that produce new substances in food. The FDA asserts the changes are negligible. But some public interest groups, such as the Health and Energy Institute, and several scientists counter that there have not been enough long-term studies to support this claim. Further, they say, there is some evidence that irradiation increases the production of a naturally occurring carcinogen called aflatoxin.

What makes matters worse, critics charge, is that the FDA proposal does not recommend that irradiated food be labeled as such at the retail level. Some comments on the proposal suggest the public might believe food so labeled to be radioactive. But Kitty Tucker, Executive Director of the Health and Energy Institute, argues that "this amounts to protecting consumers by keeping them ignorant."

The FDA says the question of labeling is still open and that it might reword the proposal. But a decision will not be made until the agency has had a chance to review all of the nearly 4,000 public comments it has received on the plan.

Garbage to Gold:

Just how should the food be irradiated? The Department of Energy (DOE) is pushing for a process that exposes food on a conveyer belt to pellets of cesium 137, a radioactive waste that can be generated from spent nuclear fuel. Tucker sees this as "a government attempt to turn garbage into gold." It would be safer, she says, to use particle accelerators or x-ray machines as sources of radiation. Unlike cesium 137, neither one needs to be transported on public highways, reducing the chance of accidental radioactive contamination.

SOMA BOARD

Can't we detoxify our food, our juices, our milk from heavy metal and chemical poisons before we put them on the table? Yes we can! It is an invention of mothers. It is a gift to the nation in trouble.

Dr. Parcells developed the Magnetic Lamp. You put all food under it, and through magnetic energy, it offsets the harmful chemicals.

I developed the Soma Board. It works like pyramid energy through transmutation of harmful elements. The two instruments in it, the blue transparent film and the herb-mineral mixture, perform the miracle.

The Soma Board is designed to bring more healthful vibrations into your kitchen. Almost all of our foods contain some kind of chemicals, additives or preservatives. These stay in your fruit or vegetables even when you wash all produce. Over the years, these additives accumulate and allergic reaction sets in. The liver just cannot neutralize so much poison.

We housewives have to do something about the additives in order to have healthy families. We have to neutralize these foreign substances which are in our food, fruit and vegetables. Otherwise, we get more and more into a pattern of poor health.

Soma is built on the idea of pyramid energy. There is no pyramid inside the box but as the pyramid energy neutralizes chemicals, so does this invention neutralize poisons and chemicals. Soma is a unique combination of minerals and herbs which achieve the ionization of your food. By doing so, chemicals and metals are ionized and will be rendered harmless.

The "Soma" treatment makes everything taste better. The fruit tastes sweeter, bread tastes fabulous, water is milder and so on. Even cigarettes change taste making it easier to quit the habit. I take mine on air flights and it neutralizes my food. Since I started using it, I don't come home with bellyaches any more.

CHEMICAL POISONING (ADDITIVES IN YOUR FOOD)

Chemical Additive	Red dye #2—Colors foods red, brown, purple and orange
Found in these Foods	Soft drinks, ice cream, cherries, candy, cake frostings
Health Risks	Has produced tumors in test animals; only the USA, Mexico and Denmark permit this additive

Chemical Additive	*Yellow dye #5*—Used to give gold-yellow color to foods
Found in these Foods	Beverages, desserts, candy, cereals, ice cream, baked goods, snack foods; also used in prescription drugs, pain relievers and antihistamines
Health Risks	Can cause allergic reactions, including wheezing, asthmatic symptoms and hives

Chemical Additive	*Blue dye #1*—Used to give a bluish color to foods
Found in these Foods	Soft drinks, gelatin desserts, ice cream, ices, dry drink powders, candy, cereals, puddings, bakery products
Health Risks	May cause allergic reactions; tests show that it produces malignant tumors in animals

Chemical Additive	*BHA (butylated hydroxyanisole)*—Prevents fats and oils from turning rancid
Found in these Foods	Cake mixes, shortenings, potato chips, breakfast cereals, gelatin desserts, candy, pudding and pie filling mixes, bakery products
Health Risks	Can cause allergic reactions

Chemical Additive	*BHT (butylated hydroxytoluene)*—Prevents fats and oils from turning rancid
Found in these Foods	Potato flakes, enriched rice, shortenings containing animal fats, frozen pork sausages, freeze-dried meats
Health Risks	Can cause allergic reactions; tests have produced chemical changes in the brains of animal offspring; England prohibits the use of this chemical in foods

Chemical Additive	*Glycerides*—Emulsifies; defoaming agent
Found in these Foods	Bakery products, ice cream, ice milk, lard, chewing gum, shortenings, oleomargarine, sweet chocolate, whipped toppings

114

Health Risks	Suspected of causing reproductive problems and malformations

---

Chemical Additive	*MSG (monosodium glutamate)*—Used to enhance the flavor of foods
Found in these Foods	Canned and frozen foods, prepared meats, pickles, soups, candy, baked goods, mayonnaise, Accent (is mostly MSG); large amounts of this ingredient are used in many Chinese foods
Health Risks	Affects nerve endings and can cause dizziness, numbness, headaches and other symptoms

---

Chemical Additive	*Nitrites and nitrates (potassium and sodium)*—Used as a color fixative in cured meats
Found in these Foods	Bacon, bologna, frankfurters, meat spreads, pickling brine, chopped meat, smoked ham, potted meats, poultry, smoked fish (including tuna, salmon and shad); some meat tenderizers are almost 100 percent sodium nitrate (fertilizer)
Health Risks	Combines with other substances to produce cancerous agents called *nitrosamines* and *nitrosamides;* can cause death by cutting off oxygen to the brain and heart

---

Chemical Additive	*Sulfur dioxide*—Prevents dried fruits from fermenting and other foods from spoiling
Found in these Foods	Wines, corn syrup, dried fruits, dehydrated potatoes, soups, condiments
Health Risks	Tends to deplete the body's supply of vitamin A; inhalation can produce respiratory irritation

115

The Natural Health Bulletin is published every other Monday by Parker Publishing Company.

Abnormal growths take many forms. The most common types are described by physicians as cysts or tumors. Tumors can be either benign (noncancerous) or malignant (cancerous). Each kind of growth suggests different kinds of imbalances in a person's chemistry. Some people are predisposed to tumor formation because of these biochemical imbalances. People with similar problems often have significant differences in their chemistry.

WHAT TO DO

Calcium

Regarding the importance of calcium to detoxify environmental poisons in the body, Prof. Drompecher and other scientists teach us the following interesting facts. A living cell needs 10,000 enzymes to function properly. To detoxify this gigantic laboratory it needs calcium. Without proper calcium supply the enzymes cannot be utilized.

Calcium also deactivates radioactive substances. It is known that radioactive material lodges in the brain easily. A proper supply of calcium protects us and screens off the foreign substances.

A most interesting book, *Nuclear Medicine,* by Dr. H. Sack and Dr. G. Legmann tells us the importance of calcium in nuclear exposure, x-rays and other ray exposures.

Prof. Dr. I. L. Nilson, University of Upsula, suggests to increase your vitamin E intake. Vitamin E is capable of neutralizing and binding carbon monoxide, carbon dioxide and environmental pollution from car exhaust.

Karma

The spiritual side to chemical and metallic poison is Karma. Karmic conditions are rare but they do exist. In this day and age it is a scapegoat and people let it go with that. Do not do that. Work hard, pray hard and the answer will come.

It is one of the seven spiritual causes of ill health. Karma is unfinished business. Many times people place their ignorance of a situation on karma. Let's be really honest.

Even if your illness is of karmic nature, work twice as hard to overcome this unfinished business. If you need help we are glad to direct you to the proper person.

Energy follows thought. This is one of the laws of the universe and we have to keep this in mind. If we have happy and constructive thoughts energy will follow these kinds of thoughts and build a healthy environment and a healthy body.

If we have thoughts of jealousy, hate, destruction, envy and fear we are inviting dark brothers and energies of the darkness. I don't mean necessarily illness but an environment in which difficulties of inner nature will appear and hinder the work you came to do in this lifetime. If you are slowed down, are frustrated to reach your goal and are hindered to express yourself creatively then you become ill.

The creative expression is the most important factor to stay well.

CHAPTER V

Worms and Parasites
as a
Cause of Ill Health

WHY DO WE HAVE WORMS?

When metals, chemicals, pesticides and environmental poisons cannot be neutralized by the liver and every function of the body goes down, then worms set in.

Worms are scavengers. Take a plant that is lacking in healthy soil. Parasites will destroy what is left of the sickly plant. The same with us. If our body chemistry is down, all kinds of worms and parasites can and will move in.

Good health starts with cleansing out the waste, including worms and parasites.

Worms and parasites are powerful contributors to ill health. Nowadays it is important to recognize worms like pinworms, round-worms and tapeworms, including the much feared dog tapeworm. It is also necessary to get acquainted with parasites from foreign countries.

Scientists know of about 120 different kinds of parasites which can invade and do invade the human body.

WHERE DO WORMS COME FROM?

The following illustration will help us: The vinegar is swarming with tiny flies. Take the vinegar away and all of them are gone. Where did they come from? Where did they go? No one knows.

Worms also need a medium to live in, just as vinegar flies need vinegar. So worms need one of the following:

1) A toxic colon
2) Chemicals or other poisons
3) An alkaline medium

Let's go back to the vinegar on your countertop. If we clean up the breeding place, the flies are gone. If we clean up the bloodstream from environmental poisons, there is nothing for the scavengers to live on. One gallon hyssop tea daily for 2 days is a terrific cleansing method for the body's toxic condition.

Worms and parasites are disturbers of balance to the entire system. Worms can cause:

120

- Mineral imbalance
- Loss of hair
- Loss of sleep
- Headaches
- Thyroid imbalances
- Intestinal gas
- Blood in stool

- Chronic prostatitis
- Allergies such as asthma
- Eczema
- Pain all over the body
- Arthritis
- High blood sugar (like diabetes)

HOW TO RECOGNIZE WORMS

An iridologist can discover parasites early but when people have coal black eyes, even an iridologist is out of luck.

Iridology is a carried down science of the blue eyed races. It was used over centuries and is still in use where blue eyed races are the majority. The American Indian looked at the soles of the feet of their people and discovered in the grooves, marks and blemishes mankind's biggest enemy—parasites.

Parasites take on the vibration of their host. Therefore, they are difficult to detect. Furthermore, I don't think it is as much what these creatures eat that is damaging to the human body but that their waste is extremely poisonous to us. A healthier environment all throughout the body is needed to discourage the existence of these scavengers and their breeding places.

If a person is very nervous at the full moon, they may have worms and/or parasites. Any treatment for worms should be done during the full moon. Worms get rampant during a full moon. They swell up.

Tapeworms create high sugar level in the blood. When there is sugar increase in urine, ask your physician for a tapeworm examination. Do not take a stool specimen on a new moon. Tapeworms and roundworms are moon animals. They sleep a great deal of the moon cycle. They wake up, multiply and get obnoxious around the full moon. Then the laboratory technician can find them.

Pyloric valve trouble: Watch for worms in the liver. Nervousness around full moon: Watch for worm infestations. Five- to seven-pound weight gain around full moon: Watch for worms. Children grinding teeth at night: Watch for worms.

121

Worms and parasites take the best of your blood and their waste is poisonous. They eat your vitamins and the more you take of them, the worse you feel. Worms do not like minerals.

TAPEWORM

When rolled up, tapeworms create a ball under the ribs of the right side below the liver. Sometimes this ball is there, sometimes it is gone. Sometimes there is an increase of weight up to 7 lb around full moon, constipation and diarrhea interchange, some people lose weight. Most people are overweight when afflicted with this problem. A tiny tapeworm has been discovered in household cats which presents a potential threat to human health. If transferred from cats to humans, this parasite can affect the liver, lungs and brain.

According to Prof. G. A. Wobeser of the University of Saskatchewan in Canada, it is the first time this parasite has been discovered in pets in North America, although it is reported to be fairly common in Europe and Asia.

"We don't know how widespread this is," Prof. Wobeser told the *Enquirer*. "We don't know of anyone dying from it, but we believe the public should at least be warned of the danger."

For tapeworms try an herbal combination of pumpkin seed, garlic, cramp bark, capsicum and thyme. Eat plenty of pumpkin seeds in all cases of worms. Weight problems and sugar imbalance are often seen with tapeworm trouble.

See also below.

ROUNDWORM

Roundworms are taken care of with herbs and herbal combinations. Also give someone with worms as much garlic as they can stand, then 2 days later give a laxative. Have them sit in a milk bath sufficient for covering the rectal area. Worms smell the milk and crawl out. Remain in the warm bath for about 1 hour until all the worms are out. This can be rather unpleasant.

Calimyrna figs have in the skin and kernels a substance which rips the skin of roundworms. It would be wise to eat some figs once in a while just to make the environment in the intestine sweet and to make it undesirable for the creatures to live.

For roundworms try an herbal combination of black walnut leaves, wormwood, guassia, cloves and male fern.

For many years I wondered where the body displayed a sign for parasitic infection. Look at the soles of your feet. I am drawing a foot chart and you can easily help yourself.

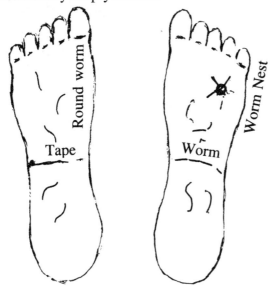

BLOOD FLUKE, ASCARIS AND OTHERS

With more and more people traveling to South America and Egypt we have come in contact with blood flukes or schistosome or bilharzia, named after the physician Theodor Bilharz.

New England I. Med. 282 270/1970 Promedico 8.8.70 Page 178. In America the stools of 201 patients with bronchial asthma were examined for parasites. In 198 patients intestinal parasites were found. Ninety percent had ascaris. Twelve patients had Strongyloides and 2 patients had Necator.

One hundred and twenty nonasthmatic patients were also examined. No worms were found. Periodic asthma attacks seem to be caused by the larvae development of the ascarides in the lymphatic system.

Pumpkin seeds are the best natural remedy against all kinds of worms. Pumpkin seeds sweeten the intestines, preventing worms to live and make nests therein.

Grate an apple, add pumpkin seeds and top with yogurt. It makes a fine breakfast for children and adults. Pumpkin seeds are not poisonous, therefore, they are of great advantage as a dewormer.

SIMPLE, GENERAL RECIPES AGAINST WORMS

General
>2 caps. wormwood
>1 caps. sage
>3 caps. capsicum
>2 times daily for 15 days

Worms in Bladder
>Black walnut
>Sassafras
>Pine needles

Worms in Tissue
>Male fern
>Yellow dock
>Black walnut
>Cloves

SALMONELLA

Try homeopathic *Ipecacuanha 6x*. In case you cannot buy it, go to the drugstore and buy ipecac syrup. Take 8 drops in water every hour, 4 hours in a row, such as 5 P.M., 6 P.M., 7 P.M. and 8 P.M. Do this for 3 weeks.

This is one of the messages the Food and Drug Administration (FDA) puts out. Two hundred and fifty thousand persons are hit annually by salmonella. People call it the 24 hour "bug" involving nausea, fever, diarrhea, stomach cramps and vomiting.

What is salmonella? It is a tiny organism which likes to live in chicken and other meat products and eggs. In its mildest form it is a nuisance. For up to 4 days you have the above symptoms. In some

124

cases, such as children under the age of 4, people who already have a weakened condition or the elderly, salmonella symptoms become a dangerous situation. Some folks are ailing with lots of stomach and intestinal trouble. Others are depressed, feverish and miserable. It can go on for years. The Department of Health and Human Sciences (HHS) cautions to wash all dishes with soap and hot water which were contaminated with raw meat preparation of a meal. Wash hands after touching raw meat and refrigerate all dairy and egg products.

Here is an herbal combination which salmonella cannot stand!

- Echinacea
- Black walnut leaves
- Russian black radish

Equal parts. Grind to powder. Fill in capsules. Take 2 capsules 3 times daily before meals.

PINWORM

Pinworms live 6 inches inside the rectum only. Take 2 cloves of garlic, mash them thoroughly, boil in 6 oz of milk, let cool and strain. Prepare an enema, inject 4 oz of this milk into the rectum. Do this for 3 nights in a row. Wait 7 days and repeat.

BLOOD PARASITE

Lately it was discovered, even announced over TV, that a hemolytic parasite (blood parasite) was found in all cancer cases. So tiny, the announcer said, that many hundred can live in a drop of blood. Very interesting. It is too bad they did not give use more help on the question: "What can we do about this?" Our Lord has the answer. He instructed us. Take equal parts:

- Natural oil of sassafras
- Natural oil of wintergreen
- Natural oil of spruce

Mix and rub 4 drops on the soles of the feet 3 times daily.

HOOKWORM

No human worm infection has attracted so much attention and has been the subject of so much investigation as hookworm. This is justifiably true, for no other worm infection is as significant to the human race as a whole. Hookworm is never spectacular like other diseases but is essentially insidious. Year after year, generation after generation, it sucks the vitality and undermines the health and efficiency of whole communities. In the course of a few summers, a healthy family may become pale and puny. Once industrious, they become languid and backward in work. Once prosperous, they fall into debt. Once proud, property owning people, they are reduced to tenancy and poverty. The children, once bright and intelligent, become dull and indifferent and soon fall hopelessly behind in school and drop out.

The Latin name for hookworm is Ancylostomatidae. There is one kind which prefers to live on the duodenum. Hookworms are small, ½ cm long or smaller, but by sucking blood they are dangerous. During World War I hookworms were treated with thymol and chenopodium oil. Nowadays, a nontoxic solution comes from England which is natural and advanced.

ANAPLASMOSIS

Anaplasmosis causes mental illness. Remedies are thyme oil and pine oil. Anaplasmosis is a cattle and sheep disease—a one-celled parasite that enters the bloodstream. Tick fever is anaplasmosis. It causes strokes and mental illnesses. The answer to tick fever is chaparral tea and 2 drops of anise oil 2 times daily.

TOXOPLASMOSIS

Toxoplasmosis was a medical mystery until just recently. Dr. Dean Jacobs, Assistant Director of collaborative research of the National Institute of Health, explained that at least 500 million people throughout the world are infected with toxoplasmosis. The parasite that caused this disease is so small that 1,000 of them can exist on a speck of dirt as small as half a dime.

Dr. B. H. Kean, chemical professor of tropical medicine at Cornell University in New York, said, "We know that any rare meat could cause

126

the infection (toxo) and now we know that cats can spread toxoplasmosis, too. Cats who have toxo spread it through their waste to anyone handling the waste." Dr. Kean and other experts estimate that 78 million people in the USA are infected with toxoplasmosis. The infection may lay dormant for many years just to break out when the resistance is low. Therefore, I quote Dr. Jacob Karl Trankel, Prof. of Pathology at the University of Kansas Medical School: "There are people who have contacted toxoplasmosis and were unscathed, but the infection lies dormant in them. An attack of the dormant parasites may be triggered when sick people are given immune suppressive drugs, to fight foreign invaders, so that the parasites suddenly begin multiplying."

Toxoplasmosis has been mistaken for other diseases for many years because so little was known about it. Dr. Leo Yercalis and Dr. Karl Frenkel say the effect of toxoplasmosis can resemble:

- Mononucleosis
- Pneumonia
- Anemia
- Leukemia
- Low blood sugar
- Brain tumors
- Hodgkin's disease
- Blindness
- Heart attack

Toxoplasmosis is, Dr. Yercalis added, critically dangerous to newborn babies. A child whose mother has the infection during pregnancy has only one chance in two of escaping the disease which may cause them mental illness, deformities and brain damage.

Eighty-six percent of low blood sugar cases have toxoplasmosis.

The answer to toxoplasmosis is: Mix sassafras oil and pine oil in equal parts. Rub 3 drops on the soles of the feet 2 times daily.

Dr. Calbert Phillips, Manchester, from Royal Eye Hospital in England, writes: Toxocara worm is a cat worm which can cause eye diseases when children or adults accidentally swallow the tiny eggs. Fever, convulsions, enlarged liver and spleen may also be caused by Toxocara worm, Dr. Phillips said.

By Jane Brody
© *New York Times Service*
New York, NY—Toxoplasmosis, the parasitic infection that contributed to Martina Navratilova's defeat in the US Open tennis tourna-

ment last month—and from which she has apparently recovered—is a far more common and often more devastating illness than most people realize.

The ultimate source of the parasite is also common: the cat. Half of the cats in this country sooner or later become infected with the parasite.

Although adults with toxoplasmosis rarely become seriously ill, an infection acquired during pregnancy can produce a highly destructive illness in the unborn child.

The result can be miscarriage, stillbirth or death of the baby shortly after birth. Or the baby can suffer birth defects ranging from mild retardation to widespread tissue destruction. Even when a baby who is infected prenatally appears healthy at birth, delayed effects from the destructive parasite can occur many years later.

Serious illness from toxoplasmosis can also occur in patients whose immunological responses are suppressed by disease or treatment.

TRICHINOSIS

Trichinosis is the name of a medically "incurable" disease in swine and humans. It is caused by a parasite, Trichinella Spiralis (trichina) and was discovered by James Paget in 1835. Encysted, you can find it in human muscle, including the heart.

Not until 1846 was trichina located as a source of trouble in swine. By 1859, scientist Rudolph Leuckart documented the entire cycle of the trichina in humans.

It is impossible to accurately estimate how many millions of human beings are infected with trichina and probably treated and overtreated for diseases they do not have. It is estimated that some 28 million people throughout the world are so infected with 21 million (75 percent) of the victims being in the USA (*Encyclopedia Britanica:* 1962, Vol. 22).

The US Department of Agriculture (USDA) provides for no inspection of pork and other meat products for the presence of trichina on the basis that it would cost too much, there being no method known other than microscopic examination. The only attempted protection is the requirement for cooking such pork containing products as wieners, salami, etc., which are often eaten without further cooking.

Symptoms are weakness, fatigue, headache, chills and fever with sweating, sore throat, laryngitis with cough and swelling around the eyes and face. Often there is a rash present on the trunk or upper extremities and/or fluid retention.

What is the answer to trichinosis? Oil of wintergreen in molasses. Take 3 drops of wintergreen oil on 1 tsp. molasses 2 times daily for 3 months. After 3 months take 3 magnesium oxide tablets 2 times daily for 3 weeks to destroy the calcium houses they had created.

Trichinosis is a disease which is completely wiped out in Europe and other countries. Statistically, it is reported that 40 percent of all lung cancer and brain cancer have their origins in the weakening of these organs by trichinosis.

How did Europe wipe out trichinosis? Trichinosis is a disease of the swine. No other animal carries it. Many religions forbade the consumption of hog meat to their followers. Mohammed forbade it, the Islams forbade it, India forbade it. All because the founders of these religions saw the great danger from trichinosis and all wanted strong men and women.

Around 1903, the health departments of all European countries met and discussed the possibility of wiping out the feared trichinosis poisoning through pork.

Germany was the instigator. Every hog that came to the market for meat was examined. A piece of the brain was removed. When there was trichinosis present, the state bought the hog at full market price so the farmer did not lose anything. Then the state went and cleaned out all the farmers' hog sheds. By and by this disease was wiped out and pork is safe to eat in Europe. There was a small flare-up after World War II when uninspected pork from foreign countries hit the markets. For a time all pork and all other animals were checked for trichinosis again. Trichinosis hits the brain of the animal first, then the lungs, then the muscles. The heart is a muscle. Trichinosis-infected animals either run in circles or are prone to heart attacks, therefore, they are sold very young in this country.

Pioneer M.D. Claims Worms in Pigs Lead to Many Deaths:

GARDENA, CA—Dr. Neil Morton, M.D., a medical electronic pioneer researching and practicing in Mexico and the US, has revealed the conclusions of research he conducted in 1969 concerning the dreaded disease trichinosis. Although trichinae are found "in everything," it is well known that pork and pork by-products are the best hosts. Until now it has been assumed that cooking destroyed the worms. However, experiments show that neither freezing temperatures nor temperatures up to 500 degrees will kill the trichinae, except after a long period of time.

However, homemakers and food handlers in butcher shops, restaurants, school cafeterias, etc., should be thoroughly schooled in prevention of the spread of this dreadful infection. If pork and pork by-products are to be used (as a calculated risk against possible infection with an incurable disease), every precaution should be taken. After handling pork always scrub the cutting board well (plastic is best) before using it for other food preparation, especially foods to be eaten raw such as salads, breads, etc. Also, wash hands well with soap and hot water and sterilize knives or slicing or grinding equipment. Butcher shops should never use the same cutting tables and equipment for pork and pork by-products as used for other meats. And, or course, be sure to cook all such products well.

Recently the Health and Human Services Department (HHS) dispatched a bulletin which stated that pork should not be prepared in a microwave oven because the microwaves will not kill trichinosis.

It should be noted that grain fed hogs carry less than 1 percent infection, compared to garbage fed hogs. The US still permits the feeding of garbage to swine and at least 6 percent of marketed animals are know to carry the infective larvae of trichina. The USDA stamp of inspection on pork is not a guarantee of freedom from exposure to this infection. Consumers should be aware of the risks involved. Government should be responsible but isn't and won't be until consumers demand the protection they are paying for.

PROTOZOA

Dr. Roger Wyburn-Mason, British medical specialist at Ealing and Houndslow Holp in West London, claims to have found both the cause and cure for rheumatoid arthritis, one of the world's most crippling diseases. He is convinced, he said, that the disease is the result of protozoan infections. Protozoa are minute, one-celled animals like the amoeba which live as parasites in the bloodstream.

Dr. Bingham, M.D., in his famous book *Fight Back Against Arthritis*, wrote:

"The presence of protozoa in the tissue can be the cause of continual inflammation in people who are genetically or otherwise sensitive to the organism."

Protozoa can cause other degeneration diseases, Dr. Bingham said, such as:

- Paget's disease of the bones
- Ulcerative colitis
- Myasthenia gravis
- Arthritis
- Chronic nephritis
- Some cases of diabetes
- Some cases of pericarditis
- Some cases of hepatitis
- Some cases of lymphoma
- Some cases of Hodgkin's disease
- Some cases of leukemia
- Some cases of ovarian cysts

What can we do? As long as you fight protozoa infection, eliminate the following foods: White potatoes, eggplant, tomatoes and red peppers.

Before each meal take:

3 tablets homeopathic *Cuprum metallicum 6x*
3 tablets homeopathic *Ipecacuanha 6x*
10 drops homeopathic *38-6*

These organisms may also cause:

- Scleroderma
- Vitiligo
- Melanoderma
- Eczema
- Psoriasis
- pyorrhea
- asthma
- chronic bronchitis
- Parkinson's disease of the central nervous system

The blood of healthy people contains antibodies against these organisms.

SPIRITUAL SCAVENGERS AND INVADERS

As parasites and worms can hurt and injure and cause great damage to the human body, so may possessions, obsessions, voodoos, curses and black magic make considerable damage to our bodies and to our lives. To protect yourself, stay in the light, pray over your children, pray over your food, send messages of love and waves of joy. Help each other and know that you are never alone.

Spastic Entities and Ailments

One of the principal effects of invading or possessing entities is to introduce spastic complaints. Entities comprise an integral part of the causation of epilepsy, spastic paralysis, cerebral palsy, etc. They are involved in some cases of high blood pressure from hypertension. They sometimes play a part in the ailment of asthma. All individuals suffering from any type of spastic symptoms should be tested thoroughly for the entire factor. Occasionally one will see an individual who suffers from voice shut offs. He or she will be talking and suddenly there is inability to get the sound out. The voice muscles in the larynx have gone spastic, invariable through the interference of entities.

Obsession in Blood Caused by Transfusions

The only published reference to this subject that I have found thus far occurs in the book *Homeopathy for the First-Aider* by Dr. Dorothy Shepherd, published by Health Science Press of England (p. 36).

Dr. Shepherd found that electronic tunings for obsession registered in the blood of individuals who had received transfusions or had given blood to others, while individuals who had never given or received blood practically never exhibited any obsession in the bloodstream. Treating the obsession out of the bloodstream brought about a decided improvement in the physical and emotional welfare of the patient.

"Blood, as the vehicle of life, is specific to each individual, containing properties peculiar to each person; aggravations and conflicts,

132

physical, mental and spiritual, are likely to ensue when foreign blood is introduced. We know not what the ultimate outcome will be, a total change of personality is likely. . . . This is too long and serious a subject to be dealt with in a few short phrases."

The vibratory disharmony created by blood transfusions creates an attraction for obsessing entities, just as a diseased condition attracts entities. When this disharmony is in the bloodstream, the invading entities associate themselves with the blood, creating the particular condition designed by the author as obsession of the blood.

What to Do

Into the category of removing subtle invasions goes the excellent work of Dr. John Ray, called the Ray Method. Dr. Ray's main work and his terrific results stem from the fact that spastic entities can be released by holding certain trigger points on the body. It is a fascinating work.

Be sure that, before you start Dr. Ray's method, you get a pulsor. A pulsor is a protective device that guards your aura against released invaders. Be sure that you pray and don't let go even if it takes hours of release work. The sternal notch seems to be the main release point.

Dr. Ray's work is so welcome since few churches take time to remove entities from their faithful and trusting parishioners. Jesus said, "Heal the sick and rebuke the dark forces."

Doctors Are Baffled by Man's Death After Voodoo Curse

Cursed by voodoo, a 33-year-old Arkansas man died of heart failure in the hospital . . . after days of living in terror.

Doctors could find no logical explanation for his death. "It was mystifying in that no medical illness was ever proven," said Dr. Roy Ragsdill, Jr., the psychiatrist who handled the bizarre case at the University of Arkansas Medical Sciences.

The uncanny death was revealed in the *American Journal of Psychiatry*. The victim, a black sawmill worker from a rural area north of Little Rock, AK, was admitted to the hospital when a nervous disorder was suspected.

"The patient had become increasingly irritable and withdrawn from his family," said Dr. Ragsdill. He was transferred to the psychiatric ward when his condition worsened.

"He became increasingly more agitated, confused and delirious. He began to have hallucinations and was terrified whenever people approached him. We put him on a high dosage of tranquilizers. That's all we could do to slow him down. But we had to restrain him."

The patient's wife told doctors that her husband had angered a woman considered to be a witch. "He hadn't paid her for her services," said Dr. Ragsdill. "It was obvious they all believed in the stuff [voodoo] and that it was very real. He could never tell us why he'd been cursed. He never really communicated at all."

The man had had no previous history of any psychiatric disorder, Dr. Ragsdill told *The Enquirer*. "To the best of my knowledge, it developed after the hex was put on him.

"After two weeks in the hospital, the patient suffered a cardiac arrest. All efforts to revive him failed. He had no history of cardiovascular disease and an autopsy provided no reason for his death.

"But this is a pattern that is reported in the medical literature of patients said to have been cursed or put under a voodoo hex. I wouldn't be surprised if that were not the main reason for this man's death."

Why does voodoo work? "If you believe in it, a voodoo hex can have impact on you," said Dr. David C. Tinling, in charge of the psychiatric consultation service and associate professor in the department of psychiatry at the University of Rochester Medical Center, Rochester, NY.

"The belief in it is all-important. We think it leads to some profound shifts in the autonomic nervous system—your inner regulating system that takes care of your vital functions."

Spirits—both good and bad—invade the minds and bodies of people who are considered mad, says a clinical psychologist.

"I have treated mental patients whose minds had been taken over by spirits," said Dr. Wilson Van Dusen. "I have examined thousands of patients and I believe these spirits were present in every single one."

Not all spirits are evil. Dr. Van Dusen said he discovered a higher order of spirits with dazzling abilities and knowledge which seemed to help and protect the patient.

134

Dr. Van Dusen, Ph.D., who was chief psychologist at Mendocino State Hospital in California for 12 years, said he has communicated with some of the spirits.

"Whenever the voice of the spirit stated, I asked the spirit questions and the spirit would give me the reply through the patient."

The evil spirits seemed to possess people who had violated their own conscience, he said.

These spirits often inflicted pain and plotted ways to kill the person they possessed, torturing the victim with threats and obscene suggestions, he added.

"Most patients reported voices that told them they were worthless and should be killed."

But Dr. Van Dusen also found kind spirits of a higher order—apparent angels that acted with great respect for the patient.

Dr. Van Dusen, who was also former associate professor of psychology at John F. Kennedy University in Orinda, CA and author of several books and dozens of scientific papers on his research, said, "It was very rarely" that he could "break through the spirits to cure a patient" through conventional psychotherapy.

"I had to go back into ancient literature on possession for help."

Prayer Action Plan for Dissolving the Spiritual Cause of a Physical Problem

The Hawaiian Kahunas used to get rid of unwanted negative attitudes and feelings by relaxing and commanding these unwanted negative attitudes to leave their bodies as they shook their right and left legs.

I suggest:

1) Review the situation that is presently causing a particular emotional stress.

2) Pick a word that expresses the positive opposite of this negative emotion (example: hate—love; anxiety—security; worry—confidence; impatience—patience; etc.).

3) Place a glass of water next to you.

4) Relax. See yourself beset with negative emotion. Put it all into the glass of water. Throw water away.

5) Take a fresh cup, preferably porcelain. Fill this cup with water and think that this water contains the necessary solution to your problem—it is filled with the opposite positive emotion. Drink the water, knowing you are filling yourself with the positive emotion you need, and the negativity will leave you when you next urinate.

6) End session. Then urinate, feeling an exhilaration of positivity.

The Healing Magic of Crystals

The most outstanding authority on crystal powers is Marcel Vogel, a senior scientist with IBM for 27 years until his retirement in early 1984. "At first this may sound paradoxical, but there are no powers whatsoever in the crystal. The crystal is a neutral object whose inner structure exhibits a state of perfection and balance. When it's cut to the proper form and when the human mind enters into relationships with its structural perfection, the crystal emits a vibration which extends and amplifies the powers of the user's mind. Like a laser, it radiates energy in a coherent, highly concentrated form, and this energy may be transmitted into objects or people at will.

"As psychics have often pointed out, when a person becomes emotionally distressed, a weakness forms in his subtle energy body and disease may soon follow. With a properly cut crystal, however, a healer can—like a surgeon cutting away a tumor—release negative patterns of energy in the body, allowing the physical body to return to a state of wholeness."

A crystal multiplies the thought form and also holds the thought form invoked in it. Therefore, a crystal has to be cleansed always before and after using it for healing or for entity removal. A crystal is a tool just as a pendulum or a dowsing rod is a tool, however, a crystal is a very delicate device. It is a tool for healing the etheric body. It is a tool for healing the aural body.

1) How do you clear and clean a crystal? I know of 4 different methods:

a) Soak crystal in saltwater.

b) Place crystal on a violet colored velvet cloth (which I have cut in the shape of a cross).

136

c) Blow at the crystal from all sides to release the thought form.

d) Place the crystal in a dish of Hawaiian red salt (this is very powerful).

After clearing and cleansing the crystal, this tool is ready to be used.

2) How can you use a crystal?

The seat of our life force energy is a point in the sternum two inches below the thymus gland. In fact, the entire sternum indicates the strength of each individual's life force. It is here at this point, close to the thymus, where we have to contact the impaired life force and heal it with the crystal. It is the point of contact, the key to the etheric body of a Western man (the key for an Easterner is the solar plexus).

a) It was taught to me in the following manner: After clearing the crystal I make 12 counterclockwise circles around the thymus gland, including the point 2 inches below the gland. Then I clear the crystal and make 12 clockwise circles over the same area. Then I hold the crystal between my eyes and give command that the crystal will send the life force for healing wherever it is needed. I hold the crystal over the thymus and command again in the name of Jesus that the etheric body of the person will be healed. When the etheric body and the aura are healed, the physical has to heal also.

b) When someone is burned do the same over the burn.

c) When someone is injured do the same over the injury.

d) If someone is possessed do it 12 times counterclockwise over the entire body. Blow the crystal over a candle flame and command the dark ones to go into the light. Then go over the body 12 times in a clockwise manner and close the energy field of the life force at the sternum either with the cross or with the directed laser beam of the crystal. I do it with the words Jesus taught us:

<blockquote>
"Tali
Tha
Cumi"
</blockquote>

"Thou shall be whole."

137

It was revealed, in newly discovered scrolls, that Jesus carried two crystals with Him, one in His right side and one in His left side of the folds of His garment.

Our Lord Jesus, Himself, gave us the words to release these foreign energies. He said; "Eph-pha-pha-open" and "Satan, go behind." Then He lifted up His head and gave thanks to His Father that it was done. And He taught this to His disciples and said: "This and more thou shall do in my name."

We are our Lord's children, His students. Let us faithfully do what He taught us to do and, in His name, we will succeed.

Pearls from the Bible for Healing

PROVERBS 17:22   A merry heart doeth good *like* a medicine: but a broken spirit drieth the bones.

ISAIAH 38:21   For Isaiah had said, Let them take a lump of figs, and lay *it* for a plaister upon the boil, and he shall recover.

PROVERBS 24:13   My son, eat thou the honey, because *it is* good; and the honeycomb, *which is* sweet to thy taste.

When bleeding is present, read: EZEKIEL 16:6 3 times: And when I passed by thee, and saw thee polluted in thine own blood, I said unto thee *when thou wast* in thy blood, Live; yea, I said unto thee *when thou wast* in thy blood, Live.

The bleeding will stop.

Three times in a row, 3 times daily, say, "By his stripes, thou shall be healed."

You will be amazed what a relief this is to you when you have pain.

CHAPTER VI

Infections
as a
Cause of Ill Health

INTRODUCTION

Since the writing of this book, science has come up with 2,200 diseases. Their names are in Latin or Greek. Some have their origin in Sanskrit. Some come from the Hebrew language. An ordinary person like you and I cannot understand this language and so we are in awe about the names of the diseases. In fact, some people come and ask, "I have a neat, rare disease. Did you ever hear about this?" Then they take a long breath and say a long word in a secret language and are proud that they could say the word and proud that they have such a rare disease. When we look it up in the medical dictionary, it may be epilepsy of unknown origin or worms in the lung.

The secrecy of this language reminds me of the churches in the Middle Ages. After Martin Luther had translated the Bible, populations of this earth were freed from ignorance. I go with the word of Christ. Know the truth and the truth shall make you free.

IMMUNE SYSTEM

Your immune system is your body's powerful defense against infections of all kinds—bacteria, fungi and viruses. As long as your immune system is working, none of these invaders can harm you.

Of which organs does this powerful system consist? As we know it now, the following organs contribute to the existence of this powerful, spiritual system: a) the thymus gland, which is the heart of your immune system; b) the spleen; c) the thyroid. What really takes place at this point, no one knows. It is suggested that the thymus gland makes and controls T cells. T cells are certain white blood cells which attack bacteria, viruses and other infection causing elements.

It is said that T cells are the bosses of the lymphocytes and also bosses of the antibody molecules. Lymphocytes are called B cells. We have 1 trillion lymphocytes which are under the command of T cells. What a job!

As we get older, the immune system becomes less powerful, less able to throw off infections. Infections in elderly people are always serious and it will take longer for them to recuperate once they have an infection.

The spleen is definitely a part of the immune system, yet, when it has to be removed because of an accident, the immune system does not collapse.

The thyroid, when properly functioning, makes thyroid hormones which stimulate the immune system. It gives spark, zest and life to the immune system. When the thyroid is under the influence of poisons this spark cannot be created.

Once your immune system fails to protect you, you are in trouble. Bacteria, viruses and fungi find possibilities to enter your bloodstream, your lymphatic system and your cells.

Infections and diseases can be harmless or very serious. We are surrounded by bacteria, virus and fungus causing diseases. We are surrounded by protozoa. We are surrounded by all kinds of diseases. Those diseases cannot harm us as long as our immune system is fit. Our immune system can be weakened by too little sleep, too much smoking or too much alcohol, by chemicals, pesticides, metallic poisons and protoplasmic poison and by ELF (extremely low frequency) waves and others.

What Causes the Immune System to Break Down?
Why Does It Fail?

The immune system suffers under the influence of chemicals, pesticides, chemotherapy, Candida albicans, the pulling of food over the scanner and radiation of all kinds (including the radiation of food for preservation).

The immune system seems to operate on an electromagnetic principle. If we supply enough specific herbs and special food supplements, we may be able to keep it working.

The following remedies are God sent for the immune system:

1) Chaparral
   Capsicum
   Goldenseal
   Echinacea

Grind up and fill in capsules or use it as an extract.

2) Vitamin A has a stimulating effect on the immune system.
3) Vitamin C foods are stimulating to spleen and thyroid.

141

4) Manganese is necessary for the thymus gland, to make it wholesome and to revitalize the immune system.

5) Zinc deficiency can cause shrinkage of the thymus gland.

6) Digestive enzymes as in pineapple and papaya are good for your immune system.

7) One of the most powerful plants to increase and balance the immune system is quaw bark, what I call the American Pau d'arco. *See below.*

Quaw Bark

Alec de Montmorency, an expert on exotic medicines and folk remedies, reportedly discovered a tree in Brazil called Pau d'arco or Lapacho. The Brazilian Indians used the inner bark of this tree in the treatment of various diseases, including tumors and cancer, with unique results.

Pau d'arco has a tremendously healing vibration for people born and living in the Southern Hemisphere where energy moves in a counterclockwise pattern. People born and living in the Northern Hemisphere where energies move in a clockwise vibration respond less favorably to Brazilian Pau d'arco.

In my diligent search for a tree with similar benefits in the Northern Hemisphere to provide special healing virtues, I consulted with the Sioux and Oglala Indians for enlightenment. They directed me to the tree which they call the quoiase or quaw tree.

Quaw bark (what I call the American Pau d'arco) regenerates cells and improves the production of red blood corpuscles. These Indians use the inner bark of the tree which they claim gives them strength, stamina and endurance and builds up the immune system.

The Indians use this bark for toxemia, varicose veins, hemorrhoids, hemophilia and tumors (including cancer). It strengthens the pituitary gland and tones the entire glandular system.

The Oglala Indians also use it to help complete the healing process of old wounds and to offset the damage done by acne. It is most beneficial when used for fungus infection of the nails, skin fungus and psoriasis.

Quaw bark definitely increases life force which may further explain why the Indians use it for longevity.

142

Another Blood Cleanser
> 1 gallon hyssop tea sweetened with honey or maple syrup
> 2 days in a row
> No food needed

Interferon

Interferon is part of the immune system. It is a product of white cells and fibroblasts and prevents viruses from penetrating body cells. Interferon is always lacking in all fungus diseases, including cancer.

Interferon is a protein, discovered and named in 1957. It is produced naturally in the body as a response to occurrences of viruses. Three different types of interferon have so far been isolated: 1) leukocyte interferon in white blood cells; 2) fibroblast interferon in connective tissues; and 3) immune interferon produced by the so-called T cells, originating in the thymus gland.

How does interferon work? It appears to function primarily as an intracellular messenger. Once a cell under viral attack produces interferon, the protein migrates through the cell membrane, spreading to other cells not yet attacked, triggering the production of antiviral proteins which are believed to block or interfere with viral reproduction.

The body produces interferon in minute quantities. One mg of interferon requires 65,000 pints of blood and it is *species specific*. Animal interferon has been achieved, hence its administration as a drug is extremely expensive.

Make Your Own Interferon

Foundation Recipe:

Put in blender of mix thoroughly by hand: 1 cup cottage cheese and 2 tbsp. walnut, almond or apricot oil. This mixture is the foundation recipe and can be varied.

1) To foundation recipe add finely grated horseradish. Serve with potatoes or buckwheat and/or stewed carrots.

2) To foundation recipe add spices, such as finely cut parsley, celery or paprika.

3) To foundation recipe add tomatoes or tomato puree to taste. This is very delicious with rice, bulgur or rye bread.

4) Make foundation recipe sweet with honey or serve it as a salad dressing.

Interferon is not only a must to stay well but, according to Dr. Uchida, interferon is used as an anti-herpes agent in man. It offsets the herpes infection.

The immune system is the mother of the lymphatic system. Without the T cells of the immune system, the lymph cannot function.

LYMPHATIC SYSTEM

The lymphatic system is extremely important. It has its own channels and disintegrates at death. When you have a hard, callous ring around your heel or foot, you have a lymph problem. The lymphatic system is pumped by movement. It does not work when you are at rest. Running and working out moves the lymphatic system. Since we have little opportunity for outdoor activity, we should have a small trampoline rebounder in our houses. Just a few minutes' workout on a rebounder 2 or 3 times daily will activate the lymphatic system which is so very needed for good health.

Our forefathers walked to work and were refreshed by arriving at work because the lymphatic system had a workout. We have to have the same—a stimulant, a workout—for our lymphatic system. So we use the rebounder, the trampoline.

Lymph Congestion

Start with 5 juniper berries a day. Chew them slowly between meals 2 times daily. Every day add 1 juniper berry so that you increase to 15 juniper berries 2 times daily. Then, every day, reduce the number by 1 until you are back to 5, 2 times daily. By chewing, take one by one. When there are 15 berries, it will take you close to 1 hour to chew so many.

Congestion in the lymphatic system is most favorably influenced by this method.

No Protein After 2 P.M.

The lymphatic system is very sensitive to protein imbalance, to amino acid imbalance and what we called "locked protein."

When you eat any kind of concentrated protein as eggs, fish, meat, cheese, soy products or fowl, it will take 8 hours to break this protein down to amino acids (the building stones of the cells), collagen, muscles and the entire body.

The liver is doing this tremendous job. After 8 hours the amino acids are ready to leave the liver to do its work. The lymphatic system is the transportation system. While you sleep, the lymphatic system is also at rest and has only a few "emergency lines" going. The building stones of your worn-out cells, the chain of amino acids, cannot reach the places of repair and dumps it somewhere, locks it somewhere, preferably in a weak spot of your body.

In case of a tumor, amino acids are dumped into the tumor. In case of arthritis, amino acids are dumped into your already stiff and painful muscles. So in case you eat heavy protein at 6 P.M., you will feed your troubles. The cancer will grow big and fat and you will starve yourself to death. You are stiff as a board in the mornings in the case of arthritis and you cannot go to work unless you flush your lymph and blood with coffee and sugar donuts.

Cell Respiration

Milk cyclone fermentation can have D-positive or D-negative aspects in the living cell. Scientists call it milk cyclone D-positive and D-negative.

The prolonged left turning cycle of D-negative milk ferment is a cause of cell deterioration. It is stopping cell respiration so that the cell nucleus forms its own entity cancer.

Dr. Engelhardt demonstrated that the heart muscle can only use D-positive milk cyclone for its electrochemical balance and strength. It is obvious that other muscles require the same for maintenance and repair. The skin is particularly thankful to D-positive foods.

D-positive milk cyclone activates the lymphatic system and detoxifies the entire body from environmental and other poisons.

What can we do to improve our defense system? What can we do to assume that D-positive milk cyclone is formed? Every culture, every nation has its own national drink or food which in one way or another is served in a fermented state.

It is the traditional yogurt of Bulgaria, Iran and Turkey, a daily drink made from yogurt and thinned down with spring water—it is the kefir. It is also the sauerkraut in Germany, the raw fish in Scandinavia; the fermented drink in South America and on and on.

We can have it all but, because of lack of knowledge, very few of us use a fermented food or drink every day.

One of the richest foods in D-positive terms is beets. Red beets are the queen of all. Just 1 tsp. of beet powder will suffice. A soup with red beets or relish made out of beets will turn the cell to D-positive. It also is a detoxifier of environmental poisons.

We had the impression that it is the color in beets which prevents metastasis in cancer but, through the biochemical and electrobio-chemical works of researchers, we find that it is the positive influences of beets to the D-negative cell that makes the miracles.

True prayers can turn the D-negative biochemcial, electrochemi-cal stream into D-positive expression and instant healing will result.

Apple Whey

> 1 qt water
> 1 qt apple juice
> 1 qt milk

Bring to a boil. As soon as it curdles, strain through a sieve. Drink first very little—6 oz 2 times daily. Then increase the quantity to 1 qt daily.

The lymph will respond. The environmental toxins will be neu-tralized.

BACTERIAL INFECTIONS

Drug-Resistant Bacteria Linked to Farm Animals:
Progress Bulletin, Saturday, July 3, 1982

BOSTON (AP)—Half of all antibiotics used in the United States are fed to farm animals, and researchers say this has led to the growth of drug-resistant bacteria that are hazardous to humans.

The 2½-year study was directed by Dr. Thomas F. O'Brien and published in Thursday's *New England Journal of Medicine.*

The study is the first evidence that bacteria are attacking humans after evolving genes inside farm creatures make them immune to common antibiotics.

These drug-resistance genes are passed from one kind of bacteria to another, and the doctors warn that they may make other common, disease-causing germs hard to kill with currently available drugs.

The doctors believe that people acquired bacteria with these genes by eating animal products, such as beef or milk.

Farmers routinely feed antibiotics to cows, hogs and other animals to prevent disease and promote growth.

Strep Infections

Thank God we have penicillin, tetracycline and other antibiotics. That we did not understand the proper care after we had to take a series of penicillin is our own shortcoming. Penicillin is a mold, a fungus. It is superior in nature to strep infection. It is more powerful than strep, therefore, it is used to combat strep infection.

The side effect is obvious. We have to take care of the side effect, of the fungus. Otherwise, we throw out Satan in exchange for Beelzebub.

When penicillin is needed, follow doctor's orders but take care of the after effects. Penicillin kills every bacteria, friendly and unfriendly, and one has to fill the void created. I suggest you do it methodically and intelligently. After you have had your last pill of penicillin, start with acidophilus. Buy 7 bottles of liquid acidophilus and take ½ bottle every day for 14 days. If you do not like the taste of acidophilus, buy some in capsules and take 3 capsules before each meal, also for at least 14 days.

A bacteria cannot enter a living cell. It will surround the cell and will multiply in the waste it creates. Therefore, large doses of vitamin C do such an excellent job by clearing the waste surrounding the cell and bacteria have to die. Penicillin and derivatives are useful because the fungus of penicillin kills the intruding bacteria but does not injure the cell. Bacterial infection can produce heart failure, therefore, consult your physician.

How do you know whether your sore throat is a strep infection or a virus infection?

- If your right shinbone is hotter than your left, it is very likely that your sore throat comes from strep infection.
- Touch your cheekbone from nose to ears. If it is sore, it is more likely that your sore throat stems from strep infection.

Here are some time proven natural remedies for those who cannot take penicillin:

- Adele Davis told us to take 1,000 mg vitamin C every hour for 10 hours when bacterial infection strikes.
- Dr. Carlton Fredericks recommends large doses of vitamin A in the same dose at the same time the first and second day. Read his books.
- Crush the pit of an avocado. Boil in 1 pt. water and take several tbsp. every hour (very effective against strep infection).
- Infection in lungs: Boil onions, mash and place between two layers of cloth. Apply to chest for about 2 hours. Repeat if needed.
- Strep infection: Grate cucumber and squeeze the juice out. Drink 5 oz 5 times daily.
- Compresses of warm milk all over the body. Wrap patient in 3 layers—a warm milk sheet, a woolen blanket and a warm cover. In 2 hours repeat if needed. Bacteria like milk better than blood.
- Take an herbal combination of black radish root and parsley leaves. This is God sent and very effective in case someone cannot take penicillin.
- Tea from linden and elderberry.
- Garlic against strep. Nature provides strep killing herbs. The number one, as you know, is garlic. Garlic's botanical name is *Allium sativum*. The use of garlic can be traced back as far as Babylonian times. The Chinese used garlic as did the Egyptians and the Romans. Garlic has the antibacterial substance allicin. It is so powerful that it is used in the battle against gram-positive and gram-negative bacteria with satisfying results.

In case your physician permits you to try garlic for strep throat, use it with sage tea, 1 heaping tbsp. sage to 1 qt boiling water. Steep it for 5 minutes and remove from fire. Add 1 tbsp. garlic juice to the qt

148

of sage tea. Gargle with it every 2 hours and also drink 4 to 6 oz several times daily. Garlic is such a potent germ killer that you will be surprised over the result.

Staph Infections
This takes an extra place in all the types of infectious diseases. Staph is difficult to get rid of once you have it.

Symptoms:

- Listlessness
- Temperatures that come and go
- Feelings of being lost
- Spells of despair
- Wounds heal slowly
- Boils break up and leave a blue surrounding which is visible for a long time afterwards
- Acne type boils on back or other places always blue afterwards

Staph infection can hide for a long time just to break out in stressful situations.

Go to a physician. Also find out about oxyquinoline sulfate (homeopathic *Oxo 6x*). This is derived from the nontoxic part of the cinchona tree whose bark yields quinine. It is a big, big help in the battle against staph infection.

Herpes II is a form of staph combined with a virus. Take all the suggestions of your physician and add oxyquinoline sulfate (homeopathic *Oxo 6x*).

Grate the skin of a grapefruit on a fine grater. Take 1 tsp. and add the juice of ½ grapefruit. Drink this 3 times daily.

Here is an interesting contribution to staph problems written in the magazine *Discovery*, August 1982.

Bugs That Won't Die:
Many deadly bacteria are now resistant to antibiotics.

After months as an infectious disease control officer at Detroit Receiving Hospital, one of the busiest hospitals in the city, Donald Levine had seen his share of tough infections. They were a routine part of the life. No matter how often the walls, floors, and bed sheets were scrubbed or boiled, disease-bearing bacteria survived and found convenient receptacles in patients already weakened by other illnesses or surgery. Levine was all too familiar with the main culprit, resistant Staphylococcus aureus, or staph, a pernicious bacterium that somehow outwits methicillin, an antibiotic designed to kill it. Fortunately, the bug is usually confined to hospitals.

The story of Detroit's super staph highlight is a growing concern in medicine. The penicillin and other families of antibiotics are fast becoming useless against many bacterial diseases.

The researcher in *Discovery* said that, overall, bacterial infection is the fifth leading cause of death in the US today. The problem is particularly acute in hospitals, where bacteria are directly responsible for 20,000 deaths a year and contribute indirectly to 60,000 more.

Discovery Reports:

The irony about the growing potency of bacteria is that man has inadvertently encouraged their resistance to antibiotics. A doctor prescribes tetracycline to a teen-ager worried about a few pimples. A woman catches a cold and figures that she may as well take a few of the antibiotics sitting in the medicine cabinet, even though she vaguely suspects they will not do much against an infection (in fact, they will do nothing). A man neglects to complete his prescribed cycle of antibiotics. Why should he take more when he already feels better? In some countries it is easy to get antibiotics without a prescription and people take them to fend off a wide range of diseases. This overconsumption and carelessness serve as a kind of natural selection process, assuring that the resistant bacteria will survive to divide and conquer later on.

Over the past year, hardly a month has passed without a drug company trumpeting the arrival of yet another brand-new antibiotic. Though these drugs are just beginning to receive the kind of broad clinical testing needed to determine their safety and effectiveness, they show great promise in defeating diseases like super staph, super gonorrhea, super pneumonia and, indeed, most of the tenacious super bugs that have appeared over the past few years. Walter Gilbert, a Nobel laureate and a professor of molecular biology at Harvard, said, "There may be a time down the road when eighty to ninety percent of infections will be resistant to all know antibiotics."

150

VIRAL INFECTIONS

Viral infections are manyfold and cannot be met with one herb or one way of dealing.

A virus has a protein coating. It has hooks. It can make enzymes which are able to penetrate the cell and dissolve its protective coating. Once inside the cell, it takes control of the host's metabolism. It will take command over the cell it invaded and will direct the cell as a unit in its own interest.

We have different kinds of viruses. Mononucleosis is one of them, flu is another one.

In my opinion, viral infections are best met with natural home remedies, such as herbs, homeopathics, baths and wet compresses.

How do you recognize if your sore throat is of viral origin in contrast to bacterial invaders? While in a strep infection the right shinbone is hotter than the left, in viral infections the left shinbone is hotter than the right. A virus turns you into a whimpering complainer. A strep infection turns you into a hot and short-tempered person.

There are home remedies for flu infections. For influenza put your beloved one to bed. As in strep infection, give lots of fluids. Make a very good tasting tea of:

> 2 parts fennel
> 2 parts thyme
> 1 part *Melissa officinalis* (lemon balm)
> 2 parts rosehip

Another good tea in all viral infections is:

> 2 parts raspberry leaves
> 2 parts nettle
> 1 part roses
> ½ part echinacea

Make a broth with white and red onions by boiling these onions in plenty of water—medium sized onions of each kind to 1 qt water. Cut onions and simmer until done. Take from fire, strain and give 5 tbsp. every hour, either straight or in more water.

Against cough:

> 2 parts thyme
> 1 part sage
> 1 part yarrow
> 1 part mullein

Sinus Infections

Take 1 tsp. honey and sprinkle with freshly ground pepper. Eat it. It is also good for the sniffles.

Also yellow onion juice against any kind of cough. Take a yellow onion, make a good-sized hole on top. Fill with honey or raw sugar. The juice released is very helpful in any cough.

I like an herbal combination of lemon peel, chamomile, thyme, capsicum, colstfoot, yerba santa, eucalyptus, wahoo bark and mugwort. The health food stores carry it. It is easy to take and most helpful.

Colds

For a cold, bad cough or pneumonia, put right hand on forehead, left hand on back of head. Hold 10 minutes for a child, then drop hands to the chest and back for another 10 minutes. Child will sleep away the illness. Also works for viral pneumonia in adults. The seat of pneumonia is in the head, not the lungs. Hold the above head posture for 20 minutes to ½ hour for an adult. It is not necessary to hold the chest for adults. Do not hold tight or press, just lay on the hands. Hand will be wet at the end of the time period. Wash them. This is the poison leaving the body.

If a fever is involved, massage or put vinegar compresses on calves of the legs to draw the fever from the head to the legs.

Spanish thyme, good for thymus gland, helps prevent colds. Take 2 cups of tea a day. Good in cooking. Add cream if children are reluctant to drink it. Can also add honey. Great beverage in winter months. For a cold or sinus congestion, go off dairy products.

Coxsackie

A physician in the town of Coxsackie, NY, found that many who suffer from pain in hip joints, hips and lower back do not have arthritis but have something caused by a virus. Most founders and inventors want their names published but this humble man called the virus after his home town, Coxsackie. This is a vicious disease. It takes a long time to manifest so that it becomes painful but there is, as far as I know, only one help. The antidote comes from Dr. Ray (England) and is called *Coxsackie* homeopathic. I am thoroughly amazed how many people suffer from this virus. It is astounding that one small bottle of *Coxsackie* antidote can take away years and years of suffering.

Measles and Mumps

Measles and mumps are viral infections and should be treated with love and care, bed rest, warmth, light food, no ice water, no ice cream, warm oil on a painful cheek and a darkened room when your child has the measles. Children after having had measles are usually stronger afterwards.

Colorado's Juvenile Diabetes Hike Laid to Flu Viruses

Several flu viruses that swept the nation last winter apparently triggered a spurt of juvenile diabetes cases in Colorado.

Dr. H. Peter Chase, a specialist at the Barbara Davis Center for Childhood Diabetes, said the incidence of new cases of juvenile diabetes is about double the usual number for the year.

"We just don't have a national perspective on this," he said. "We don't have a good system of diabetes reporting."

Chase said that two particular "bugs"—coxsackie virus and respiratory syncytial virus—may be responsible for the local diabetes outbreak. By themselves, they normally aren't serious. But when they infect a youngster with an inherited tendency to develop diabetes, they may provoke the disease.

"It is known epidemiologically that we get new cases [of diabetes] whenever viruses go through the city," said Chase. "The current belief is that there is a genetic predisposition, a hereditary factor in the disease. If a child has that and the right virus comes along, he ends up with diabetes."

Mononucleosis

A virus in the lymphatic system is widespread. You are tired, listless, sleepy, dull and depressed. It can be with you for a long time and it is so easily taken care of with herbs.

- 1 qt of red raspberry tea daily.
- Also, an herbal formula of raspberry leaves, basil and lettuce will soon relieve you from this trouble.

Be sure you take herbs long enough. Mononucleosis goes into hiding just to break up when you don't need it.

Arthritis

Dr. Douglas Baker from England brought the news to America that most arthritis, osteoarthritis and rheumatism have a hidden virus. In England they found that a dog virus is responsible for these pains. In this country the herbal antidote is a combination of yucca, black walnut leaves, yellow dock, wormwood and fenugreek seed. It is used to straighten out the damage.

This dog virus can be dormant for many, many years, just to break up whenever resistance is low.

Multiple Sclerosis Linked to Pet Dogs

Medical researchers say the mysterious cause of multiple sclerosis (MS), the nerve destroying disease that afflicts more than 250,000 Americans, could be the family dog.

Dr. Stuart D. Cook, who is chief of the department of neurosciences at the College of Medicine and Dentistry of New Jersey in Newark, headed a team that investigated the possible link between dogs and MS.

In two separate studies, he surveyed 74 MS patients and matched them with people of the same age, sex and socioeconomic level who did not have MS.

He found that 65 of the 74 patients had house dogs, while only 43 of the 74 MS free people had them.

Dr. Cook reported the findings of his studies involving MS patients in the prestigious British medical journal *Lancet* and in the American Neurological Association's *Annals of Neurology*.

Dr. Cook's research team also found:

- MS patients are more likely than other people to have house dogs in both the 5- and 10-year periods before the onset of the disease.

- In MS victims, close exposure to pet dogs before their illness begins is extremely high.

"These results suggest that exposure to house pets may sometimes be associated with subsequent MS," Dr. Cook concluded.

Dr. Cook pointed out that distemper virus causes neurological damage in dogs, similar to the nerve tissue destruction in human beings with MS. But he said the findings also hold out hope for preventing MS.

Answer: *M.S.* homeopathic drops from England.

Simian Virus 40

The biggest tragedy that ever hit America started in the late 1950s. It came like a shooting star, brilliant and beautiful. It raced from coast to coast touching almost every home. Then it disappeared. But, unlike a shooting star, it left behind a trail of sorrow, despair, mental and physical illnesses, suicide, financial ruin for many families, confusion and the "hippie" problem.

It was the Salk Vaccine, the most extensive experiment on humans ever performed, and it became the biggest disaster ever known to mankind.

In the late 1950s thousands of little rhesus apes were shipped to America. They were delivered by the truckloads to laboratories. With long needles their little kidneys were pierced and the deathly polio virus was injected. The little animals became deathly ill, the kidneys decomposing with pus and decay. On the heights of their suffering the rhesus apes were killed and the pus extracted. This was injected into fertile eggs and after a few days, the famous Salk Vaccine was ready to be injected into our children's bloodstreams. Many vaccines are made that way, however, here entered the tragedy. The polio virus was dead but no one knew and no one checked that, with the vaccine, a little virus slipped in which is only known to be present in apes.

This ape virus has the scientific name of simian 40, in short sim 40 or SV40.

Sim 40 is harmless to apes but when entered into the bloodstream of our children, the disaster started.

The big business, the huge propaganda machine, the praise and the advertisement subdued the cries of the parents whose children were suddenly hit with:

- Fear
- Lack of cleanliness
- Anguish
- Failing physical health
- Failing mental health
- Depression
- Laziness
- Hatred towards parents and teachers
- Low-grade temperature
- Listlessness
- Meningitis

. . . and many more behavioral symptoms which were not present before the vaccine was given. Many physicians realized very soon that something went wrong with the inoculations. To avoid more troubles for their patients they injected sterile water until they knew what was going on and the propaganda machine became occupied with other things. It was Dr. Sabin whom God gave the wisdom, stamina and integrity to help us. Dr. Sabin also bought rhesus apes. One of his first helpers was bitten by an ape and this man developed a strange fever. It looked just like a brain fever but it was much more and carried many of the symptoms the parents noticed in their children. Dr. Sabin found sim 40 in his associate. Then he examined the Salk Vaccine and in each vial there was this ape virus.

Sim 40 had never been in the human blood before and all at once millions of Americans had it. Of course, many children were able to throw the virus off. But many of them, particularly the fine nerved ones, the sensitive ones, were unable to cope with it. No one understood why these children behaved so strangely. They became loners, they were chilled, cold, miserable. They became paranoid, fearful and depressed and developed suicidal tendencies. Soon they forgot to wash themselves or comb their hair and did not care about their appearances and then the parents had to throw them out of their houses because it was a disgrace to see them in society.

In the streets they found company—boys and girls their age who understood what fear was. They all had the chill, they knew how terri-

156

ble it was to be alone when the suicidal tendencies struck. They knew how the deep depression could hit and hurt.

Up in the mountain valleys they kept to themselves in flocks like sheep do. Two slept in one sleeping bag because of fear to be alone, because of fear of the incredible nightmares and because of the chills they went through night after night.

Many of these people are now between 30 and 45 years of age. Many have seen the horror of mental institutions. Many committed suicide. Many have seen jails from the inside and many just exist.

The acute stage of this virus is over, however, it is not dead. The second episode is showing up. Many, many children, also folks between 40 and 60—senior citizens who never had had the first inoculation of polio vaccine, the one which brought the tragedy—now have sim 40 in their system. It hides in the spinal fluid, in the nervous system, and they feel tension in the back of their necks and between the shoulder blades. According to medical textbooks, veterinarian textbooks and the research done at Colorado University, sim 40 is an RNA/DNA virus. That means it goes into the nervous system. It is the most feared of all types of viruses because it can stay dormant for many, many years just to strike whenever the system becomes low in energy.

One clairvoyant said, "I feel death in many people, right in their necks and between the shoulders." Sim 40 may break up any day now and it is that which the Bible quotes: "When two stand in the fields, one will be taken."

Year in and year out, in despair, I searched and researched every avenue open to my simple mind and understanding. I prayed for my own children and my beloved ones in the mountains and streets and the ones in despair all over this beautiful country. I asked for a vision to help us. He said: "My people are dying from lack of knowledge." And I believe so deeply that I asked Him for His knowledge. And Jesus the Christ, in His grace, reached down to us and gave in a vision the help we need so badly. Formula:

½ lb. basil
½ lb. kelp
1 lb. milk sugar

Grind up the herbs and mix together. Take 1 tsp. 4 times daily in water, juice or yogurt for at least 6 weeks. I have noticed that some people have a light fever for a few days but most people feel better right away for the first time in years.

Also, a homeopathic product from England under the name *22-44* is a miraculous help.

Since it is a hidden virus, it may come and go for a while but keep on taking the formula. See your children regain their mental and physical stability. See yourself changing to better health. All who read this, please become a missionary for the Lord and for this nation's health.

Twenty-four years have passed and sim 40 virus is still on the warpath. One of the factors leading to AIDS is sim 40. Spindle cell cancer is another one.

I had a most unusual meeting with a physician from Switzerland. For a while she was the right hand of Dr. Albert Schweitzer, the "Saint of Lambarene" (African).

During the evening we talked about the hippie movement and I told the incredible story of sim 40. I had finished. The 80-year-old woman jumped to her feet, grabbed my shoulders and said, "Say this once more. It cannot be, it cannot be." I asked her why she was so excited and she answered, "Being with Dr. Schweitzer was the most incredible experience of my life. He helped everybody, he took everyone in, he treated animals, birds and what not with utmost admiration for life itself but when someone was bitten by an ape, he sent those people back into the jungles to die while tears ran down his cheeks. Ape virus, sim 40, he said, is a nerve virus. It settles in the RNA and DNA. It is also so dangerous to human blood that I cannot take the risk to have these people on my premises. *Sim 40 is still the pain in the neck.*"

(SCIENCE 7 April 1972)

"There can be few graver opportunities for manmade disaster than the mass immunization campaigns that are now routine in many countries. Should the vaccine preparations become contaminated with an undetected agent present in the host cells, such as a cancer-causing virus, a whole generation of vaccines could be put in jeopardy. This, of course, is no science fiction writer's horror story—it has already happened once; millions of people have been injected with a monkey

158

virus known as SV40, which was found in 1961 to be contaminating polio and adenovirus vaccines. The virus causes cancer in hamsters; no one yet knows what it may do in man."

Viroids

An entirely new field of infections is the newly discovered tiny virus called viroid.

Viroids can be 80 to 150 times smaller than a virus. Viroids are ring shaped. They have, in contrast to a virus, no protein shell but force themselves into a living cell. Viroids are able to give orders to the cell nucleus to make thousands of their kind.

It is entirely possible that viroid is latent in the cells and it just breaks out when the environment is right. It is possible that the so called "slow viruses" are indeed viroid. It is suggested by scientists that viroids may be in Alzheimer's disease, in nerve deterioration, in MS and in other slow progressing diseases. It is reported that viroid diseases are closely related to intron and the disease appearance is very similar.

Where do viroids come from? Are they genetic accidents or normal components of a healthy cell that escape and pirate the cells of another species?

No one has answers yet. But the speculations of viroid researchers lead them onto the frontiers of molecular biology—a rapidly evolving study that has lately revealed a surprisingly active and changeable life cycle for the nucleic acids RNA and DNA, which carry the genetic code. Biologists have found that these long-chain molecules often split apart and rearrange their internal parts. Theodor O. Diener, who coined the term viroid, speculates that the tiny pathogens are a kind of genetic fallout from this process.

Can the human body harbor viroids? Yes, we can house these mystery agents.

The difference between a virus and a viroid is the following: Viruses have protein coatings. Once a virus finds its way inside a host cell, the virus takes control of the host's metabolism. It then orders the cell to build 1,000 more viruses. In contrast to a virus, a viroid has no protein coating. Because of its minute size, it can squeeze into a cell even without a protective coating. It is naked, as scientists say.

159

A viroid is so small that it cannot create or build an enzyme. Hans Gross of the Max Planks Institute in Munich was the first scientist to work out the genetic code of a spindle tube, a viroid. He surprised us with the most profound knowledge. A viroid (spindle tube) can contaminate a whole field of potatoes by hitching rides on tractor drawn cultivators and then being brushed off onto other plants. Viroid diseases also are found in chrysanthemums. Called chloratic mottle, it also can destroy the citrus industry. This viroid is called *exocortis* viroid and has done much damage.

Mr. Diener, an outstanding specialist on viroids, believes that viroids exist innocuously in some healthy plants, in tissue in tubes, just to become active for reasons unknown.

Viroid researchers see no reason why some baffling animal and human diseases might *not* be caused by runaway fragments of RNA and DNA, which are viroids.

Scientists suspect it is possible that viroids can linger harmlessly in cells for years after infection, only to flare up inexplicably. We think of possible Alzheimer's disease or other slow progressive brain and spine disorders. At the present time, the viroid and its use for war germ techniques are studied intensively.

A viroid infection can be sudden also. You feel fine one day and the next day you feel as if you are two persons in one. Some people have double vision, most people feel very ill and some have backache. For some, the articles in the room sway back and forth. It can be expressed in many ways. Seldom is this invasion accompanied by a fever. Therefore, it is shrugged off and you name it as unimportant, that you must be overworked, mentally deranged and so on.

Viroid can become a new cancer in our lives. It is still not known what triggers the smiling cat into a vicious lion. Could it be the fallout? Could pollution, chemical saturation or sodium fluoride be bringing new and crippling diseases? Scientists are studying and with the help of God they will find the answer to a viroid antidote in plants and humans.

Viroids can express themselves in:
• Lymphoma
• Leukemia
• Norwalk virus

- Meningitis (spinal)
- Meningitis (brain)

What to do:

1) A *Viroid* powder containing:

   Gelatin
   Rice polishings
   Whey
   Glutamic acid
   Basil powder

   Take 1 tsp. 2 times daily in 1 glass of juice or water.

2) This is the best: Take 2 leaves of an aloe vera plant. Wash them and cut them finely. Cover them with water, 1 cup aloe vera to 3 cups water. Bring to boil and simmer for 15 minutes. Add ½ cup honey and simmer 5 more minutes. Take from fire, let cool and put through a strainer. Give 2 tbsp. every hour to an adult and 1 tbsp. every hour to a child. You may dilute it with water. The healing power seems to be in the green covering of the plant. It is excellent.

Viroid infections have a tendency to eat up your vitamin B_{12}, therefore, you become very tired during and after the infection.

FUNGAL INFECTIONS

A medical doctor has recently stated that a problem of the future will be fungus. This is not a problem of the future, this is a problem now. This is a very common problem here in the US and many are plagued with it. Many lung problems are caused by fungus infections.

Candida Albicans

One of the most feared of all infections is the fungus infection. Over 2,000 years ago, Hippocrates described an oral and vaginal thrush which we know now as a fungus called *Candida albicans*.

Normally, *Candida albicans* is confined to skin and mucous membranes but nowadays, because of the general breakdown of our immune systems, candida can invade the bloodstream. Once in the bloodstream, it expels a powerful poison against the nervous system.

161

Symptoms of Unrestrained Candida Albicans

Unrestrained *Candida albicans* occurs when this fungus takes off all at once. *Candida albicans* overgrowth means that this fungus has entered the bloodstream and no longer nests on membranes of mouth or intestines.

Here are some of the many symptoms when you are in trouble:

Generalized:

- Fatigue
- Joint pains and stiffness
- Cold hands and feet
- Increased body hair
- Numbness and tingling

Gastrointestinal tract:

- Chronic heartburn
- Gastritis
- Colitis
- Distention and bloating
- Gas

Some symptoms, according to Dr. William Crook, that may suggest a yeast problem:

In children:

- Hyperactivity
- Recurrent respiratory tract infections
- Recurrent ear infections
- Neurological and behavioral symptoms

Often symptoms occur following sugary meals or snacks, when none have been handled successfully or diagnosed in traditional ways.

In adults:

- Depression
- Extreme sensitivity to common chemicals like perfumes or tobacco smoke
- Persistent vaginitis
- Prostatitis

- Digestive symptoms
- Hives
- Psoriasis and other skin problems
- Headaches
- Lack of coordination
- Premenstrual syndrome
- Dysmenorrhea
- "Feeling bad all over" for no apparent reason
- Impotence
- Persistent jock itch
- Athlete's foot and fungus growth on nails

When the poisonous effect of Candida albicans hits the central nervous system, we are in deep, deep trouble. The fear of losing the mind is real and many have suicidal tendencies and so on.

- Headaches
- Depression
- Lethargy
- Hyperirritability
- Memory loss
- Inability to concentrate

These are just a few of the signs that the fungus *Candida albicans* has come to its final stage.

Nerves in collision, due to the fungus *Candida albicans*, is a common daily occurrence. It is a serious problem. It is a paramount problem. Fifty percent of people in mental institutions suffer acutely of this fungus infection. From 169 adults studied, 163 had *Candida albicans* overgrowth.

In everyone's guts we will find *Candida albicans* but a healthy body keeps *Candida albicans* in its natural limits and it will not harm. We still ask questions. Why did our Lord put this in our intestines in the first place? There must be a reason. There must be something good that a restrained *Candida albicans* fungus does for us.

Bob, a teen-ager, had a serious acne problem. The only thing that helped him was tetracycline. He had taken it for 2 years with only minor pauses in between. The acne subsided but had left huge scars in his face. I met him when he was 20—depressed, shy, leaning towards

163

drinking, cold hands and feet, complaining of stomach trouble, bleeding ulcers, bleeding from bowels and, at times, tremendously restless.

For a minor incident in a bar he was sent to Canyon City, a penitentiary. Because of his restlessness and depression he was placed in a crawl space where he could not stand up or walk but just lie back or sit on the floor. After 3 weeks in that dungeon he had to be put into the hospital chained to his bed.

Released, he never found his way back. He was a plumber (and a good one) but he did it without joy or enthusiasm. The money he made he used for the only relief of his depression—dope. He died of an overdose, 8 hours before his little son was born. Cause of death: *Candida albicans*, the fungus caused by tetracycline in his teens.

Diet and Lifestyle when Candida Albicans Hits

1) Eat a low carbohydrate diet. Buy a carbohydrate guide so you can keep track of your carbohydrate intake.

2) Avoid antibiotics and steroids unless absolutely necessary.

3) Ladies, do not use the birth control pill if you fear this problem. The pills upset your hormones, thus interfering with your body's ability to fight candida.

4) Take up to 3 tablets or capsules of acidophilus and/or bifidis each meal.

5) Use garlic. If you cannot eat the whole garlic, take an odorless garlic supplement.

6) At least 30,000 IU of vitamin A should be used for the first 2 weeks of this program. Thereafter you can cut the dosage down to 25,000 IU per day. (Use the emulsified form of vitamin A for the high dosage segment. It will not accumulate in your liver.)

7) A substance sometimes called B_{15} also seems to be effective. We have found Organic 15 to work very well.

8) Approximately 2 weeks into the program, add 2 tablets per meal of raw thymus, a glandular tissue.

9) Quaw bark tincture to uplift immunity system.

10) Zinc tablets at a strength of 15 mg each have been found useful by taking 3 to 6 daily.

11) An herbal combination of white pine bark, mugwort, myrrh, chamomile, catnip and mullein, 1 with meals.

12) Exercise at least 20 minutes daily.

13) Moderate sunlight is beneficial to kill candida overgrowth.

14) Drink 5 ounces marjoram tea 2 times daily.

15) A combination of condurango bark, yellow dock and red clover is an herbal antidote to *Candida albicans*. This should be taken with an herbal combination of tansy, clay, milkweed, cramp bark, goldenseal leaves and blessed thistle.

16) Avoid all yeast products.

17) Reduce your intake of refined carbohydrates and alcohol.

18) Avoid brewer's yeast, raw mushrooms, chocolate and other sweets.

Fungus in Lungs

Cases of fungus in lungs are more and more frequent. Fungus is like a mushroom. When you cut a batch of mushrooms, 2 days later a new batch is growing a few yards away. The feelers, the spores, just grow a new batch. The same holds true with a batch of mushrooms in your system. We call this metastasis.

What to do to change your chemistry so that fungus will be discouraged to grow? Change your diet.

What Is Cancer?

"Cancer is a disease of the RNA/DNA structure of the cell," the medical books tell us. "Cancer is not a single disease but a group of many diseases with a common characteristic; uncontrolled, invasive growth at the expense of normal body system, but the basic cause of cancer is unknown," they conclude. Not so. We know that cancer is a fungus disease and in rare cases it is a spindle cell viroid.

Since cancer, in most cases, is a fungus disease, we have to look at which foods and herbs are antifungal in nature. Fungus is a mushroom. Look to nature. (*See* "Fungus in Lungs," *above*.)

Never toss away the helping hand of a surgeon who is able to remove a cancerous growth. But try not to let it come to such an event, such a tragedy. In case it was necessary to remove the growth which you did not know existed, have a surgeon remove it. Do something afterwards. Change your lifestyle again by cleaning the fungi from your body. Do something against metastasis: Eat 50 percent raw food, 50 percent cooked food and *NO* protein after 2 P.M.

What follows is an electromagnetic diet.

THIS IS IMPORTANT

Electromagnetic Food Combining

1
- All sea food
- Whole eggs
- Lamb
- Beef
- Potatoes, white
- Potatoes, sweet
- Eggs
- Veal
- Oyster
- All fish
- Olive oil
- Rutabagas
- Tomatoes, fresh
- Tomatoes, cooked
- Green pepper
- Rice
- Oils

2
- Spinach
- Avocado
- Watercress
- Okra
- Beets
- Radishes
- Parsnips
- Salsify
- Lettuce
- Sauerkraut
- Kohlrabi
- Beet tops
- Dandelion
- Brussels sprouts
- Peppermint
- Broccoli
- Green peas
- Cauliflower
- Carrots
- Green corn
- Onions
- Cress
- Green beans
- Cabbage
- Escarole
- Asparagus
- Pumpkin
- Cucumbers
- Chard

3
- Sweet milk, raw
- Yogurt
- Cream
- Filberts
- Tea, lemon
- Gelatin
- Bread, whole grain
- Steel cut oats
- Cereals
- Cornmeal
- Maple syrup
- Almonds
- Wheat germ
- Goat's milk, raw
- Buttermilk
- Cheese, natural
- Butter
- Cottage cheese
- Millet
- Rice
- Bread

4
- Cherries
- Apricots
- Peaches
- Pineapple
- Grapes
- Plums
- All berries
- * *
- Bananas
- Melons
- Molasses
- Brown sugar
- Preserves, honey
- Raisins
- Dates
- Figs
- Pomegranates
- Currants
- Rice, brown

5a
- Lentils
- Beans, dried
- Mushrooms
- Peas, dried
- Eggplant
- Peanuts

5b
- Grapefruit
- Lemons
- Limes
- Watermelon

5c
- Cooked or canned
- Tomatoes
- Spaghetti
- Rice
- Corn
- Millet

Combine 1 and 2

Combine 3 and 4

Combine 5a with 2
+Corn
Rice
Millet
Greens above ground

Combine 5c with 2

Apples and rice are universal

166

- No more fried, greasy foods
- No more TV dinners
- No more aluminum pots, pans and foil
- No more soft drinks or beer from aluminum cans
- No more protein after 2 P.M.
- No more pastry and sugar products
- Food has to be 50 percent raw and 50 percent cooked

To change body chemistry fast, drink 1 gallon hyssop tea sweetened with honey or maple sugar for 1 day. No other foods. If at all possible, do it 2 days in a row.

Another method is the Seneca Indian cleansing diet which also changes the chemistry in a hurry. *See* Ch. III (Congestion as a Cause of Ill Health: Seneca Indian Cleansing Diet).

Which Foods Are Antifungal?
- Asparagus: 2 tbsp. cooked asparagus (can be canned) 2 to 3 times daily.
- Alfalfa sprouts: Very good to stop cancerous growth.
- Almonds: They have B_{17} in them.
- Onion: Parboil and use in salads and foods.
- Macadamia nuts: Rich in B_{17}.
- Seeds: Such as flax seed, chia seed, sesame seed and clover seed.
- Grains: Such as oat groats, barley, buckwheat groats, millet and rye.
- Beans: Such as lentils, mung beans and chick peas.

Which Herbs Are Antifungal?
The famous Mr. Hoxey was watching his sick horses going to a certain spot in the meadow and picking only certain herbs. They went to his herb rich patch of the meadow 2 times daily. The rest of the day they munched on grasses and whatever the farmer had to offer.

From this crude beginning, and through Mr. Hoxey's keen observation, the following terrific formula came on the market. You can buy the ingredients yourself or buy the ready-made pills available in health food stores.

167

Hoxey Formula:

Red clover blossoms	Cascara sagrada bark
Chaparral	Sarsaparilla
Licorice root	Prickly ash bark
Pokeroot	Burdock root
Peach bark	Buckthorn bark
Oregon grape root	Norwegian kelp
Stillingia	

Also, an herbal combination of alfalfa seed, blessed thistle and goldenseal root is a powerful herb food combination often used with and after antibiotics. It is a fungus infection transmuter.

Combine it with an herbal combination of yellow dock, cramp bark, yarrow, milkweed, plantain, organic tobacco and tansy, which acts as a blood cleanser.

To reduce the "feelers" is the next job. (This recipe is used in Europe.) Take 1½ cups milk. Add 2 tbsp. dried calendula petals. Bring to a boil and simmer for 10 minutes. Strain it. The herb milk is 1 day's supply.

Take 2 tbsp. at a time every 2 hours or more often. By night you should have emptied the milk mixture. Do this 3 weeks in a row. Every morning make a new day's supply.

Fungus on Toenails or Fingernails

Take kerosene and add camphor (available in drugstores as a white block). Chop camphor block into kerosene until saturated and paint nails with this solution 2 times daily. After 1 week, nails look differently.

I want to introduce to you the outstanding work of Dr. H. Budwig, Germany. This lady doctor gave us practical help through her book *Is Cancer a Fat Problem?*

She said, "Cancer patients have to eat and starve the tumors." She takes raw cottage cheese called "quark" and adds cold pressed oils to it. With this the starved cells are supplied with an oxygen rich product. Her findings coincide with Dr. Szent-Györkis' research, even though they never met.

Both precious physicians say that certain proteins can carry electrons which are vital for the health of the starving cells. With raw oil,

Dr. Budwig adds another important factor, "Vitamin F," which also becomes an oxygen carrier to the starving cells.

Make Your Own Interferon

See Immune System: Make Your Own Interferon, also in this chapter.

Self-Examination Taught in England and Denmark:

Sterilize a pin. Prick 1 fingertip. When the blood comes with a pearl, you are healthy. When it smears, change your diet and lifestyle.

When the drop runs and more than several drops come out from 1 prick in a thin stream, have an examination by a doctor, change your diet, get well quickly and thank God for this knowledge.

Self-Examination Taught in America:

Put part of your morning urine in a smooth plastic cup. Cover it with one thin layer of tissue paper and set in a dark place, as under the sink or cupboard. At bedtime set cup in your refrigerator on the lowest shelf, way back so that no one else touches it. Next morning pour urine out. If you have a fungus in your system there will be a fatty, waxy rim where urine and air met.

This is an early examination which you can do for yourself.

Leukemia

Leukemia does not have the characteristics of a fungus disease. Prof. Brauchle in Dresden taught and demonstrated the following: "I want to illustrate to you the cause of leukemia," Prof. Brauchle said. "Here is my little dog. Take a blood sample and examine it. Then treat the dog badly for one week. 'Get out of here,' scold him, turn him away but give him food as before." After one week the dog had leukemia. The next week we were to be kind to him and love him. No extra food was permitted. When his blood was tested no leukemia was found. Prof. Brauchle taught us this lesson with the remark, "The same it is with humans." Some children do not get enough love, others are rejecting love and both are heading for leukemia.

169

What did Prof. Brauchle do?

We had to prepare an egg fruit drink. We also had to stroke the children from head to toe lightly, ever so lightly, hardly touching the body. I was amazed to learn that this is not done all over the world.

1 pt. freshly squeezed orange juice
1 pt. freshly squeezed grapefruit juice
1 pt. water with the juice of 3 limes
1 pt. water with the juice of 2 lemons
1 pt. frozen pineapple juice, diluted
1 pt. papaya juice, diluted
1 pt. grape juice
12 whole eggs
6 egg yolks
Frozen raspberries or strawberries add a delicious flavor

Beat eggs and mix into fruit mixture. This is 1 day's supply. For a child, ⅓ to ½ of the above amount.

The beating of the eggs and egg yolks seems to be very important. Eggs prepared this way will remove avidin from the stomach.

What Is B_{17}?

B_{17} is not a newcomer. It has been used for a long time. Researchers found B_{17} in over 1,000 plants. In bitter almonds and apricot kernels it is present in the most concentrated form but millet and all seeds show B_{17} in appreciable amounts.

The Chinese used bitter almond tea for tumors as far back as 3,500 years ago. It has been used in the Eastern world for centuries as an extract, a tea and an infusion. In Turkey apricot kernels are combined with figs and eaten as a special treat for cancer sick folks.

The Greeks and Romans used bitter almond water medicinally and called it *Amygdala amara*. As early as 1845, Fedor Inosemozov, the Russian physician, combined bitter and sweet almonds for two kinds of "fungus-like tumors."

In the year 1830, the chemists Robiquot and Boutyron isolated B_{17}, called amygdalin, in its pure form. Only 7 years later, in 1937, the scientists Liebig and Woehler discovered that amygdalin is split by an enzyme complex into:

1 molecule of hydrogen cyanide
1 molecule of benzaldehyde
2 molecules of sugar

Commercially, B_{17} is called laetrile and a tremendous fight and dark cloud is over this one word.

Laetrile has two aspects when specially fabricated. The laetrile from Mexico has a positive male vibration and the laetrile from Germany has a female vibration.

I suggest that you make your own B_{17}, which is cheap and most effective, and it also has both male and female aspects, therefore, the body can and will pick up the vibration it needs.

Here is your homemade B_{17}:

4 apricot kernels
2 pieces dried apricots
5 tablets *Calcarea carbonica 6x* homeopathic or limewater

Chew this. Take the formula 2 times daily. It tastes wonderful!

COLOR HEALING

LET THERE BE LIGHT . . .

The pineal gland converts light energy into an electrochemical impulse which feeds directly into the hypothalamus. The hypothalamus is filled with chromophilic (light sensitive) cells which convert the electromagnetic signal of light into a neurochemical impulse. This is then carried directly to the pituitary gland. The pineal gland acts as a general synchronizing, stabilizing and moderating organ on behalf of several physiological processes.

In the New Age, healing will be done through music and color. Music and color have been used throughout history by the Egyptians, Hebrews and Greeks.

Color healing is a tremendous uplift to the immune system and lymphatic system and an antidote to inflammations and infections. Color healing is gentle and very effective. It becomes yet a greater tool if color healing is applied with music—not music as we think of with loud voices and many instruments.

171

Attributes of Spectro-Chromo Colors

Red   Stimulates the nervous system which energizes sight, smell, taste, hearing and touch.

Stimulates and energizes the liver and builds hemoglobin.

Makes you feel warm and energetic and expels poisons from the system through the skin.

Orange   Stimulates the lungs, a lung builder.

Stimulates the thyroid and relieves cramps and muscular spasms.

Brings stomach glands to work properly and relieves flatulence.

Best of all, corrects bone softness and rickets and helps calcium to be absorbed properly.

Yellow   Stimulates the motor nervous system which energizes the muscles.

Helps the lymphatic system which becomes sluggish due to the scanners in the grocery stores.

Stimulates bile production and influences pancreatic enzyme output. Therefore, it increases bowel movements.

Increases peristaltic movements and even makes worms and parasites so uncomfortable that they leave.

Is used in melancholia because it functions as an equilibrator by balancing portal circulations.

Lemon   Works by being a cerebral stimulant. Therefore, it favorably changes the process of nutrition (assimilation) and can repair persistent, old disorders.

Is a bone builder by bringing phosphorus into action.

Is a thymus stimulant and can become a good expectorant when mucous is congesting lungs and bronchia.

Green   Is a pituitary stimulant.

Influences muscle and tissue building.

May dissolve blood clots and should always be tried when clots are forming.

Destroys bacteria, viruses and viroids.

Acts as a germicide and disinfectant.

Prevents decay and is a fine cleanser.

Turquoise *See* Blue.

Blue	Is a pineal stimulant, therefore, it builds vitality.
	Reduces fever (febrifuge).
	Removes inflammation.
	Relieves itching and is very soothing to the nervous system.
	Relieves burns and is cooling and refreshing.
Indigo	Is a parathyroid stimulant, therefore, it makes calcium available to the nervous system and herewith acts as a tranquilizer.
	Checks the flow of blood because more calcium is freed to act on blood corpuscles and platelets.
	Is a pain reliever.
	Eases suffering caused by grief, excitement and uncertainty; in all, it is a sedative.
Violet	Is a spleen stimulant.
	Builds white blood cells to defend against infections.
	Decreases overstimulated muscular activity (hyperactivity) and also calms down overactive heart muscle.
	Is a lymph gland depressant which comes in handy in mononucleosis or other lymph diseases.
Purple	Increases the function of the veins.
	Lowers blood pressure by dilating the blood vessels, reducing heart rate and helping the kidneys.
	Reduces fever and makes you less sensitive to pain.
	Induces relaxation and gives you deep sleep.
Magenta	Is an aura builder. It stabilizes emotions.
	Stimulates heart, kidney and adrenal gland.
	Increases circulation and makes you feel happy.
Scarlet	Contracts the blood vessels, therefore, it increases blood pressure.
	Is helpful during the time of delivery because it tends to expel the fetus easily.
	Increases kidney functions.

Color and Sound

When color is used just as a color, it is to the body like a day without a breeze. The color cannot penetrate to stimulate, let us say, the pituitary or the kidney because there is no sound to guide the color deeper into the respective organ.

When you use sound it has to be the sound of one melody performed by one instrument, such as one voice or one viola or one cello or one violin. If an orchestra is played with the color healing it would have an effect on the body as if a duck went into the water. The aura will close and the well intended music will not heal and will not bring the color to work.

This is what you do: Buy solo pieces or sing yourself. Make your own recording in the following way:

Color:	Sound (music piece) in:
Red	G
Orange	A
Yellow	A#
Lemon	B
Green	C
Turquoise	C#
Blue	D
Indigo	D#
Violet	E
Purple	A#
Magenta	G and E
Scarlet	G

I remind you: Color healing should be accompanied with the sound of one voice or with the tone of one violin or one cello. No wonder that the lullabies we sang to our children were so soothing, so effective. One sound brings colors into the aura. Sound and color will be the future healing therapy.

Chapter VII

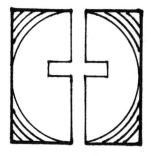

Miasma and Residue
as a
Cause of Ill Health

"The knowledge about that which we know is only
a fraction from that which we do not know."

"He who supplies another with a constructive
thought, has enriched him forever."

Alfred Armond Montepert

MIASMS

Miasms are carried over diseases which have their genetic origin in long past forefathers. A miasm can be traced to four and five generations before you. The disease pattern is not the same as the original disease but tends to be very hard to be treated with conventional or non-conventional methods. I know for sure of three distinct miasms.

1) Tuberculosis (TB)
2) Syphilis
3) Gonorrhea

Nowadays people speak of cancer miasms and others. Remember, a miasm has its origin way back but expresses in this lifetime in a completely different form.

TB miasms express themselves in:

- Scoliosis.
- Hammertoe.
- Bunions.
- Enlarged, painful finger joints which we call arthritis.
- Generally, miasm carriers have weak lungs but hardly ever manifest tuberculosis.

Remedies:
T.B. Residue homeopathic, rubbed into painful areas and taken by mouth.

Also, lupus seems to have its origin way back and is helped by taking *T.B. Residue* and *Thuja occidentalis* homeopathic. It takes up to 3 years to interrupt this miasm.

Syphilis miasm goes still further back. As all miasms, it skips a generation or two to appear in skin lesions, general weakness, psoriasis and dementia. *Syphonium* homeopathic is the answer.

Gonorrhea miasm is the least serious one and good nutrition is the factor indicated here.

INOCULATIONS WHICH LEFT UNDESIRABLE RESIDUES

Tetanus Constrictive nature, particularly in babies (crybabies).
Measles Nerves in spine and trouble in spinal fluid; MS.
Mumps Female cysts and most often a cause of prostrate trouble in later life.

Mumps and measles residues can be carried over from childhood when these diseases are not cared for in a proper manner (warmth, rest and love). The virus can hide and strike mercilessly when men and women are in their primes of life.

In this category go the hidden subtle poisons which mankind has to deal with.

Black Widow Nerve poison.
Brown Spider Nerve poison.
Dog Bite Convulsions, even years and years later.
Rattler Of constrictive nature, often in throat, producing constant cough or heart pain.
(which can be in milk, cheese or meat from an animal bitten by a rattlesnake)

YOUR TOOL: THE PENDULUM

The first time I learned about the pendulum was through Linda Clark, famous author on nutrition. In her book, *Get Well Naturally*, she describes how her friends used the pendulum and there is where it all started for me. I took my wedding ring and hung it on a thread, dangling it over my hands, my knees and my food and, sure enough, slowly, slowly the ring started gyrating. I steadied myself in every way possible but the ring was moving.

For one year I worked on this phenomenon, not showing it to anyone but my closest friends. I ordered books printed in England, France and America. I found writings in the Bible about it. I talked to prominent women, to doctors, to psychologists, but no one could give me the answers I was searching for. Why does a pendulum work? What energies are involved? And many more questions.

ABOUT VIBRATIONS

We live in three worlds of vibrations.

I

The first manifestation of vibration is physical and expresses in:

- Feeling
- Subsonic sound
- Audible sound
- Supersonic sound

The media through which these manifestations are transmitted are:

- Gas
- Liquids
- Solids

The speed of transmission through this media is 1,100 feet per second (fps) in air.

Physicists and scientists have instruments to measure the physical existence of the above vibrations.

II

The second manifestation of vibration is electromagnetic in nature and expresses in:

- Low frequency electrical
- Radio broadcast
- High frequency radar
- Infrared
- Ultraviolet rays
- Cosmic rays

The medium through which these vibrations are transmitted is the ether.

The speed of transmission through this medium is approximately 185,000 miles per second.

It was in 1975 that scientists declared that the human body has an electromagnetic system with circuits and outlets. Above mentioned vibrations use this electromagnetic system. Even though it is possible for the scientists to measure the above mentioned vibrations outside the body, it is not possible as yet to measure these frequencies in the human body with the conventional methods and conventional instruments.

The human body has organs which transform the electromagnetic waves so that the impact is buffered. These organs are the holy chakras. There are 9 chakras in a Western man and 7 in an Eastern man.

III

The third manifestation of vibration is astral-etheric in nature. It is called *Higher Dimensional Energies*, in short HD, and expresses in:
- Aura emanation
- Eloptic emanation
- Meditation
- Prayer
- ESP (extrasensory perception)
- Emotion
- Thought

The medium through which these vibrations are transmitted is *Akasha* or *Nieonic*.

The speed of transmission through this medium is instantaneous.

To measure astral-etheric vibrations, physicists and chemists, including biochemists, are not equipped to do so. They do not have the proper instruments to measure etheric vibrations. Even the De La Warr's Radionic Instruments need an operator with well developed ESP.

Intuition comes from a higher realm. Intuition is the language of the soul. If you could find an instrument with which you could ask your soul directly, would that not be a fantastic invention? Such an instrument exists. It is the pendulum with which you can converse with your all knowing soul. (Your soul is always in connection with higher intelligence—with God.) You ask your soul with your pendulum and you will receive the answer through your pendulum.

Some scientists will admit that there are aura emanations. Some will admit that there is power in mantras and power in prayers. However, scientists do not have an instrument which will measure the output of an earnest prayer. There is no gadget that can measure a prayer in numbers or weight or angstroms. Therefore, scientists may deny the existence of these powers. They may deny the reading of an aurameter, a psychometric reading, and will ridicule the use of a dowsing rod.

Many people say that what scientists cannot measure does not exist. That is not so. The foundation on which science stands is the rational materialistic realm. The prayer of a soul and the purity of a heart are fields beyond rational, materialistic view. They are realms of a higher nature.

In many states of the US radiesthesia is still a public no-no. This is hard to believe since radiethesia is widely and publicly used in France, England, Germany and Russia. In particular, France, with her great son and pioneer Abbe Mermet, is way ahead in psychometric knowledge. And yet, it is in America where the greatest breakthrough into the realization of these astral-etheric vibrations was made. Scientists found that the nerves are the transmitters of vibrations mentioned in section I above. In 1975, the electromagnetic web below the skin was recognized to be able to transmit energies mentioned in section II above.

In 1908, researchers at Harvard University came up with astounding news. They found that certain energies enter our bodies through the pores of the skin, go through endless nadis or channels and gather in 33 centers. I want to make sure that we understand that these higher energies are not electromagnetic in nature, they are not using the chakras as transformers. They are finer in nature. These energies are true healers.

Through these nadis and centers the intuition flows. As I stated, the intuition is the language of the soul and the pendulum, the rod and radiesthesia are the instruments with which you can measure and verify and interpret the language of your soul and come in contact with the all knower.

At Harvard, the research was dropped since they had no practical use for it.

Chapter VIII

Collection
of
Knowledge

    This chapter contains an odd collection of knowledge gathered over the years.

    I hope that you enjoy it as much as I enjoyed compiling it.

SOLOMON'S SONG
(Solomon 4:14)

Spikenard	1 tsp.
Saffron	2 pinches.
Calamus	¼ tsp.
Cinnamon	2 sticks
Frankincense	¼ tsp.
Myrrh	¼ tsp.
Aloe	¼ tsp.

In approximately 7 cups purified water, add herbs and boil 15 minutes, simmer, put in a glass jar and refrigerate.

Drink 2 cups daily for 3 days. (Do this once a month—every month—to cleanse and take out impurities from the body.

BODY SIGNS

Left ankle swelling	Heart problem
Right ankle swelling	Kidney problem
Sprained ankle	Emotionally ungrounded
Large hips	Pituitary gland
Over muscular legs	Rigid personality; will not change easily; firm in beliefs
Under muscular legs	Depends on others for support
Right shoulder pain	First heart chamber trouble
Left shoulder pain	Entire heart is in trouble
Throat problems	Liver problems
Continued sore throat	Restrained anger
Stiff neck	Prolonged tension
Hemorrhoids	Liver problem; holding on to all feelings too long and too tight—let go

Taste or Appetite Changes May Be Warning Signals

If you notice an unusual, persistent change in your taste or appetite, it may be nature's way of warning you that something it wrong with your body. Here are descriptions of the more common changes in taste and appetite and of the problems that may underlie them.

• *Sour taste or a persistent craving for tart fruits:* May indicate difficulties with the gallbladder or liver.

• *Bitter taste:* May suggest vitamin and mineral deficiencies or colitis.

• *Craving for sweets:* May signal the development of hypoglycemia or diabetes, not enough protein or Candida albicans infection.

• *Craving for spicy foods:* May indicate difficulties in the lungs or sinuses.

• *Dislike for meat or taste loss:* May indicate cellular distress and possibly cancer. Many stomach cancers are associated with the symptoms of unpleasant taste and a dislike for meat. This may also be caused by a lack of hydrochloric acid. Taste loss may indicate a zinc deficiency.

An occasional craving or unusual taste is no cause for alarm. However, if the change is persistent, bring it to the attention of your physician.

Eyes
You amazing eyes do more than just see. They can reveal important things about your health, experts say.

• If one pupil is larger than the other, it can indicate that a tumor is hidden somewhere in the body.
• Red eyes can signal an infection in the eyes that is usually caused by a virus or bacteria. Red eyes can also be caused by allergies or air pollution.
• Changes in vision, such as being able to see better on one day than another or seeing double, are warning signs of diabetes. If you already know you're a diabetic and experience these symptoms, it may mean the disease has not been properly controlled.
• If the whites of the eyes turn yellow, it can be a sign of hepatitis, a blockage of the gallbladder duct or the presence of a tumor in the pancreas.
• Difficulty reading, even while wearing the correct glasses, may point to thyroid trouble.

• Being able to see better on cloudy days or in the evenings than on bright, sunny days or seeing a rainbow or halo around glowing streetlights are possible signs of glaucoma.

• Vision that wavers between clear and blurry can be an indication of high blood pressure.

Don't treat yourself. Let a competent medical authority confirm the problem.

Seven Pulses for the Western Man
1) Lazy—weak or dropped kidney
2) Pounding—artery hepatic
3) Wiry—inflammation
4) Fast—coxalgia plexus
5) Intermittent—phrenic nerve
6) Pounding with expansion—abdominal aorta
7) Jumping—pancreas and liver

Legs
If the left leg is short, take a cloth drenched with vinegar. Place it over your forehead and it straightens out at once. If the right leg is short, place soda on the forehead. Reason: Sympathetic nervous system is supposed to be an alkaline medium, parasympathetic nervous system in an acid medium. If this is not in order, the length of the legs will change.

To recognize an acid condition: Dehydration, lump in the throat and dry skin.

To recognize an alkaline condition: Itching, stiffness, night cough, night cramps, sensitive and overweight below the waist.

SCIENTIFIC BREATHING: A TIME SAVER
Lower Abdominal Breathing
Make circles of the index fingers and thumbs and extend other fingers straight out and close together. Place hands palms down on groin. Elbows should be at right angles to your body. Breathe deeply. The breath will be confined to the area below the navel.

186

Intercostal Breathing

Make circles of index fingers and thumbs and fold remaining fingers into the palm. Place hands palms down on groins. Elbows should be at right angles to your body. Breathe deeply. This breath will be felt in the lower abdomen and up to the area under the ribs.

Utilizing Upper Clavicular Area of Lungs

Make baby's fists by folding 4 fingers on each hand over thumbs. Place fists on groin and breathe deeply and slowly. This breath will fill your entire lungs.

AMINO ACIDS: WHAT THEY DO

Histidine
Pineal—right and left side
Pancreas—right and left side

Homocystine
Pineal—right and left side

Aspartic Acid
Pineal—right and left side

Leucine
Pancreas—right and left side
Elbows

Asparagine
Pancreas—right and left side

Tryptophan + Carnosine
Pancreas—right and left side

Tyrosine
Lower jawbone

Phenylalanine
Liver, jawbone left side

Isoleucine
Heart + left side

Phenylalanine
Vagina—right and left side

Glutamic Acid
Lung left side + brain right side

Serine
Lung right side

Cystine
Liver—left side

Proline
Liver—left side

Alanine
Liver—left side

Methionine
Liver—right side

Gamma-Aminobutyric Acid
Kidney—right and left side

Glycine
Kidney—right and left side

Hydroxylysine + Norvaline
Spleen—right and left side

Lysine
Spleen

COFFEE

Personally, I am not in favor of coffee. However, I am asked over and over what coffee does. Like every plant, it does something to the system. What follows is a list you might enjoy to read.

Do not use milk in coffee because it crystallizes to gallstones, kidney stones and hardening of the arteries.

Sugar in coffee is a no-no also. But a little bit of honey in coffee makes the difference. When I need an extra lift after 10 hours of work and I have to be alert for another 4 hours, I take ½ cup of coffee with a little honey in it and, zoom, I can go!

It is also important to know when taking coffee enemas what kind of coffee will do what. All coffee beans stimulate pineal and pituitary and are extra good in enemas when cancer has hit. Some coffee beans stimulate the spleen and some stimulate the pancreas.

Always remember, a little coffee goes a long way. It can be a strong remedy if chosen properly.

Colombian	To rectum—up to stomach gland—to heart (extra good)
Guatemalan	To rectum—to pineal—to coccyx—vitamin B_6
Mexican Maragogipe	To duodenum—pepsin—pineal
Kenyan	Pancreas—grape sugar
Hawaiian Kona	Kidney—beryllium
New Guinean	Spleen—sex (male–female)—folic acid
Mexican	Pineal—cortisone to heart—cystine—iron
Peruvian	Larynx
Salvadorian	Tongue—borax soda—quartz crystal
Continental Roast	Appendix—gypsum—calcium
Viennese Roast	Pituitary—cobalt—quartz—salt
Colombian Supremo	Pineal—grey lime—insulin
Jamaican	Pineal—liver—heart—element B_2
Costa Rican	Liver—manganese—B_{12}
Nicaraguan	Pineal—magnesium—citric acid—vitamin E
Mocha	Pineal—bone ash—iron—cobalt
Java	Colon and rectum—vitamin C—digitalis—lime phosphate
Ethiopian	Liver—radiation mineral Liver—electrical magnetic
Indian	Spleen

SPECIFIC HEALING PROPERTIES IN FOODS

ANISE	For flatulent conditions.
APPLES	Whatever ails you: gallbladder trouble, liver trouble, diarrhea, tooth decay, constipation, loss of appetite; good as poultices, too. When someone is very ill, take an apple and scrape the meat with a silver spoon. You will see them return.
APRICOTS	Detoxifies the liver and pancreas.

189

ASPARAGUS	For fatty tumors and the like. Helpful in urinary secretions.
AVOCADO	A fat and protein supplier. Good for the diabetic.
BARLEY	A calcium supplier, colon aid and lymph cleanser.
BEANS (ADZUKI)	For kidney trouble and swollen ankles.
BEANS (GREEN)	Remove metallic poison. Good for the malfunctions of the pancreas.
BEANS (LIMA)	Make a dish with lima beans, bell peppers and sweet potato to combat drug residue.
BEANS (RED)	Build muscles. Served with corn, a complete protein.
BEANS (WHITE)	For the eyes and for liver trouble.
BEANS AND CORN	Muscle builders (especially red beans).
BEEF	Muscle food.
BEETS	Spleen food.
BELL PEPPER	Eyes and digestion (increases pepsin).
BLACK BEAN JUICE	For hoarseness and laryngitis.
BLACKBERRIES	Colon food. For diarrhea.
BLACKSTRAP MOLASSES	A mineral and iron supplier.
BLUEBERRIES	Pancreas food. For sugar problems.
BLUEBERRY AND BANANA	Pancreatitis.
BUCKWHEAT	For energy and warmth. For strong muscles.
BUTTERNUT	Liver food.
CABBAGE	For vitamin U, the tissue builder.
CARROTS	Eyes, blood and lymph.
CELERY	A low calorie reducing aid.
CELERY SEED	Drink the tea for obesity.
CHERRIES	For gout.
CHERRIES (SOUR)	For gout and as a blood cleanser.
CHICKEN	A gland food.
CHICKPEAS	A gland food. Good protein. An antiviral, particularly anti-polio virus.

CRAB APPLE	For vertigo.
CRANBERRY	A kidney food. Releases sudden cramps as in asthma and the like.
CUCUMBER	A skin remedy, kidney cleanser and infection cleanser.
CURRANTS	Build resistance to colds. For anemia.
EGGPLANT	Give the peelings and dulse to the afflicted tumor.
FIGS	A dewormer.
FISH	Good protein and iodine supplier.
GARLIC	Carbohydrate residue in tissue and glands.
GRAPEFRUIT	A lime supplier. A flu destroyer.
GRAPES	Antitumor, good for anemia and an aura builder.
INDIAN CORN	Perfect food for man. Has all the energies, amino acids and hormones the body needs.
KALE	For resistance to colds.
LEEK	For reducing. A pancreas food, tissue builder and brain food.
LEMON	Vitamin C.
LEMON (WHITE OF RIND)	Bioflavonoid. Strengthens tissue.
LENTILS	Iron. Contains protein supplies of the best quality.
LIME	For yellow jaundice.
MEAT	Lots of calories. Protein that gives an explosive energy. Appetite satisfying.
MILLET	Meat of the vegetarian. Fifteen percent protein.
OATS	Brain food.
OILS, COLD PRESSED	Needed to assimilate the proteins from vegetables. Also a kidney food.
OKRA	Regulates female bleeding. Gives strength to leukemic patients.
OKRA AND APPLES	For ulceration of the stomach.
ONION	Make a soup of fresh red and white onions and collards for the flu.
ORANGES	Vitamin C for flu prevention.

PAPAYA	For protein digestion.
PARSLEY	For piles.
PARSLEY ROOT	For kidneys. When boiled in white wine it is for the heart.
PARSNIP	For intolerance to milk.
PEACHES	Good during pregnancy.
PEARS	Kidney and colon.
PEAS	Green and dried peas are good sources of protein and good for weak stomachs.
PINEAPPLE	Enzyme supplier.
POMEGRANATE	A dewormer.
POTATO PEELINGS	For kidney ailments.
POTATOES (RED)	For stomach and duodenal ulcer.
PRUNES	Iron, constipation.
PUMPKIN	Spleen and pancreas food.
PUMPKIN SEEDS	Dewormer, parasites.
RADISHES	In small amounts, promote bile flow.
RAISIN	Anemia, blood builder.
RHUBARB	Colon cleanser.
RICE	Universal acceptance by all tissues (overrated at the present time).
RICE GRUEL	Diarrhea.
ROMAINE LETTUCE	Virus infection.
RUTABAGA	Food for prayer. Feeds friendly bacteria in colon. Once a week it would be good.
RYE	Muscle builder.
SAUERKRAUT	Keeps old folks' ailments away.
SESAME SEEDS	Complete amino acid supplier. Makes strong willed people. Supplies osmium, a trace mineral.
SPINACH	Good for you if you have anemia.
STRAWBERRIES	A skin berry.
STRAWBERRIES AND SQUASH	Remove metallic poisons, especially arsenic.

SUNFLOWER SEEDS	Feeds eyes, sinuses and glands.
SWEET POTATO	Gland food.
SWISS CHARD	Arthritis (contains Wulzen factor).
TOMATO	As poultices in deep rooted afflictions. When stewed, good for liver. Fresh tomatoes are a vitamin C supplier. Green tomatoes in very small quantities are a gland stimulant. Always remove the core of the stem. Make a deep insertion. This stem part is poisonous.
TURNIPS	For deep rooted tumors. For deep rooted resentments.
WATERCRESS	Supplier of vitamins C and E.
WATERMELON	For sluggish kidney and a kidney cleanser.
WHEAT	Starch and calorie supplier.
YAMS	Hormone food.
YOGURT	Intestinal health.

RECOMMENDED READINGS

The following books are available at Hanna's Herb Shop, 5684 Valmont Road, Boulder, CO 80301, (303) 443-0755.

The Healing Benefits of Acupressure
By Rev. Dr. Fred M. Houston, D.C.

Flouride: The Aging Factor
By John Yiamouyiannis

The Yeast Connection
By Dr. W. Crook

Fight Back Against Arthritis
By Dr. Robert Bingham

About the Author

Hanna Kroeger

"One who sees this dynamic blur of activity in her store or at home, responding to piles of mail, working on a new book, inspecting herbal blends and caring for her family must wonder, 'Does she ever rest?!!'"

This spry and cheerful woman is ablaze with important tasks. Her continued accomplishments in the field of natural health care are astounding. Hanna Kroeger was born in Turkey, the daughter of German Christian missionaries. Her childhood was full of fascinating experiences, as her parents ministered and helped others with whatever means they had available. As a young woman, she attended nursing school at the University of Freiburg which trained nurses for work abroad. Later she assisted Professor Brauchle at a large hospital in Dresden which primarily used natural healing methods. It was here that she began to discover many amazing ways to restore health using herbs, special diets, baths, massages, etc. This hospital helped many people using these natural methods.

After the war, Hanna and her family moved to the United States, eventually settling in Boulder, Colorado. In 1958, she opened one of the first health food stores in the country. She named it New Age Foods because she envisioned the world moving into a new time of peace and health. There are many laughter filled stories of those early years in the store. She recalls how customers reacted when she began selling wheat germ. They asked why she would sell "germs" and whether these "wheat germs" would make you sick.

Her knowledge of herbs and natural healing developed rapidly as she continued to research and experiment with herbs and home remedies at her inexhaustible pace. She has always been an avid reader, keeping up with contemporary nutritional and medical knowledge.

Local folks began to visit her little store regularly, interested in how to stay well naturally. She shared her insights with them. As the years went by, word spread and people from all over the country could be found waiting in her store to have a few moments of her time. Many stories were exchanged by those waiting to see her, often about the remarkable results of these methods. She taught classes in her health cafeteria upstairs from the store. To accommodate out-of-

195

state students she began to hold three-day workshops at her home, the Peaceful Meadow Retreat. She taught kitchen remedies, first aid, food combining and, of course, how to identify and use herbs.

During these early years Hanna's students made their own herbal combinations. She gave them her favorite recipes, many originating in Europe or from American Indian culture, and many of her own formulas. She is a master at using the subtle and unique properties of combinations of two or more herbs to improve whole systems of the body. The students would track down the herbs, measure and mix them and put them into capsules. They were elated with the results! Later, with encouragement from her students and friends, Hanna began to have these herbal formulas milled, blended and encapsulated by a local herb company and made available at her health food store.

In 1978 she began her own herb company, Kroeger Herb Products. Her company succeeds in maintaining the highest standards for the formulas. Hanna personally inspects each blend of fine herbs. Kroeger Herb Products is now carried by health food stores and practitioners all over the U. S. and internationally.

Over the years Hanna has written many books on health, emphasizing her "common sense" approach to achieving health. She believes that God can heal any ailment, at any time, and that it is up to us to seek and apply an action that will provide an avenue of healing, such as nutrition, herbs or spiritual methods. Hanna has developed a fine reputation as a lecturer as well. She travels across the U.S. in the spring and fall, sharing her vast knowledge of achieving wellness. She has spoken at health conventions across the U.S. on a vast array of subjects. She spends her summers at her home in Boulder, teaching students from all over the world, including many from the health care field.

Hanna advocates freedom of choice in health care, hoping that people will retain their freedom to choose natural methods of attaining health as well as modern medical methods. She wishes to see the two factions working together, the best of both worlds, so that people can choose which treatment is best for their needs. Her intuitive wisdom has been a blessing to those whose lives she has touched. She has devoted her life to helping people improve their wellness. Her advice to all of us is to be open to try things and see for ourselves what does and does not work. Her life is a fine example of her simple and powerful message to humanity: "Help each other."

*BE STILL AND KNOW THAT
I AM GOD.
WHEN I REFLECT ON THIS STATEMENT,
WHEN I BECOME OUTWARDLY AND
INWARDLY STILL,
WITH IT COMES THE GROWING FEELING
THAT GOD IS HERE — AND WITH GOD
ALL THINGS ARE POSSIBLE.
I GIVE THANKS FOR THE PRIVILEGE
AND ABILITY TO WIPE OUT THE PAST
AND CREATE A NEW LIFE, BY LIVING
IN ACCORDANCE WITH THE LAW.
". . . FOR THE FORMER THINGS ARE
PASSED AWAY . . . BEHOLD,
I MAKE ALL THINGS NEW. . . ."*

Revelation 21: 4, 5

*May the
angels of love
heal you.*

Hanna

Peaceful Meadow Retreat

You are invited . . . .

to participate in the upcoming

NATURAL AND VIBRATIONAL HEALING SEMINARS

If you would like to learn how to help yourselves and others with exciting new healing methods, then these weekends are for you.

Learn unusual healing techniques from Hanna Kroeger, well-known lecturer and author of many books.

You will be taught the seven physical and spiritual causes of ill health and about such diseases as Candida albicans, Epstein-Barr and hidden nerve viruses which lower the immune system, MS, Alzheimer's disease and many others.

- Amazing discoveries in natural healing.
- The best learning vacation you ever had.

Rev. Hanna Kroeger
7075 Valmont Drive
Boulder, Colorado 80301
(303) 442-2490 or 443-0755

Books by Hanna

"Wholistic health represents an attitude toward well being which recognizes that we are not just a collection of mechanical parts, but an integrated system which is physical, mental, social and spiritual."

Ageless Remedies from Mother's Kitchen
You will laugh and be amazed at all that you can do in your own pharmacy, the kitchen. These time tested treasures are in an easy to read, cross referenced guide. (92 pages)

Allergy Baking Recipes
Easy and tasty recipes for cookies, cakes, muffins, pancakes, breads and pie crusts. Includes wheat free recipes, egg and milk free recipes (and combinations thereof) and egg and milk substitutes. (46 pages)

Alzheimer's Science and God
This little booklet provides a closer look at this disease and presents Hanna's unique, religious perspectives on Alzheimer's disease. (15 pages)

Arteriosclerosis and Herbal Chelation
A booklet containing information on Arteriosclerosis causes, symptoms and herbal remedies. An introduction to the product *Circu Flow*. (14 pages)

Cancer: Traditional and New Concepts
A fascinating and extremely valuable collection of theories, tests, herbal formulas and special information pertaining to many facets of this dreaded disease. (65 pages)

Cookbook for Electro-Chemical Energies
The opening of this book describes basic principles of healthy eating along with some fascinating facts you may not have heard before. The rest of this book is loaded with delicious, healthy recipes. A great value. (106 pages)

God Helps Those Who Help Themselves
This work is a beautifully comprehensive description of the seven basic physical causes of disease. It is wholistic information as we need it now. A truly valuable volume. (196 pages)

Good Health Through Special Diets
This book shows detailed outlines of different diets for different needs. Dr. Reidlin, M.D. said, "The road to health goes through the kitchen not through the drug store," and that's what this book is all about. (90 pages)

Hanna's Workshop
A workbook that brings together all of the tools for applying Hanna's testing methods. Designed with 60 templates that enable immediate results.

How to Counteract Environmental Poisons

A wonderful collection of notes and information gleaned from many years of Hanna's teachings. This concise and valuable book discusses many toxic materials in our environment and shows you how to protect yourself from them. It also presents Hanna's insights on how to protect yourself, your family and your community from spiritual dangers. (53 pages)

Instant Herbal Locator

This is the herbal book for the do-it-yourself person. This book is an easy cross referenced guide listing complaints and the herbs that do the job. Very helpful to have on hand. (109 pages)

Instant Vitamin-Mineral Locator

A handy, comprehensive guide to the nutritive values of vitamins and minerals. Used to determine bodily deficiencies of these essential elements and combinations thereof, and what to do about these deficiencies. According to your symptoms, locate your vitamin and mineral needs. A very helpful guide. (55 pages)

New Book on Healing

A useful reference book full of herbal, vitamin, food, homeopathic and massage suggestions for many common health difficulties. This book is up-to-date with Hanna's work on current health issues. (155 pages)

New Dimensions in Healing Yourself

The consummate collection of Hanna's teachings. An unequated volume that compliments all of her other books as well as her years of teaching. (150 pages)

Old-Time Remedies for Modern Ailments

A collection of natural remedies from Eastern and Western cultures. There are 20 fast cleansing methods and many ways to rebuild your health. A health classic. (105 pages)

Parasites: The Enemy Within

A compilation of years of Hanna's studies with parasites. A rare treasure and one of the efforts to expose the truths that face us every day. (62 pages)

The Pendulum, the Bible and Your Survival

A guide booklet for learning to use a pendulum. Explains various aspects of energies, vibrations and forces. (24 pages)

Spices to the Rescue

This is a great resource for how our culinary spices can enrich our health and offer first aid from our kitchen. Filled with insightful historical references. (64 pages)